Parent Power:

The Key to America's Prosperity

Why do we permit babies to have one, two or three strikes

against them at birth and endanger our nation's future?

Jack C. Westman, M.D., M.S.

Cataloging-in-Publication Information for this title is available
from the Library of Congress.
ISBN: 1482381966
ISBN 13: 9781482381962
Library of Congress Control Number: 2013903403

CreateSpace Independent Publishing Platform
North Charleston, South Carolina

Printed in the United States of America

Dedicated to

Nancy Kathryn Baehre Westman

Table of Contents

Acknowledgements

Without the encouragement and editorial assistance of my wife and life companion, Nancy Kathyrn Baehre Westman, I could not have written this book. Without the experience of raising three sons, growing affection and respect for three daughters-in-law and participating in the lives of nine grandchildren, I would not know firsthand the vicissitudes and the rewards of parenthood.

My work with systems that affect children and families over five decades brought me together with professionals from a variety of disciplines. I am especially indebted to Norma Berkowitz, Paul Brandl, Glen Cain, Tom Corbett, Jack DeWitt, Ethel Dunn, Marty Fliegel, Vern Haubrich, Jim Hickman, Margo Melli, Frank Newgent, Dave Nordstrom, Gary Ranum, Tom Schleitwiler, Florian Smoczynski, Bernie Stumbras, Bob Sundby, Jan Van Vleck and Sherwood Zink. Through the nonprofit organization Wisconsin Cares, Inc., we are devoted to stimulating awareness of how struggling families affect their members, their communities and society as well as to strengthening those families, many of which began with adolescent parents.

I am grateful for the editorial assistance of Alison Carlson and Laine Cunningham.

I am most grateful to the children, teenagers and adults who have permitted me to share their lives in clinical and organizational settings. When I refer to a specific individual or a family, I have altered names and identifying circumstances to protect their privacy. When information about persons is in the public domain, I have used actual names, situations and places.

For ease in reading I have not given detailed references for the scientific work upon which this book is based. At the risk of being repetitive I also have reiterated key points throughout the book.

Preface

The Gross Domestic Product measures everything
except that which makes life worthwhile.

ROBERT F. KENNEDY
UNIVERSITY OF KANSAS, MARCH 18, 1968

A baby's smile warms our hearts and draws us in. We human beings are hardwired to care for newborn babies for the survival of our species. Yet more than eleven million of our children in the United States were born to parents who damaged them by neglect and/or abuse. An example of their fates is the Cradle to Prison Pipeline outlined so well by the Children's Defense Fund. Why do we permit babies to have one, two, or three strikes against them at birth and endanger our nation's future?

The most obvious reason is that we act as if we do not know that parents have the power to enhance or detract from our nation's prosperity. We leave the future of our children with parents who are unwilling or unable to raise them to separate professions and social services that try to help these struggling families but cannot deal with the obvious causes of intergenerational poverty, crime and welfare dependency. What's more, these unconnected, crisis-recoil responses to problems cannot apply what we know really works to prevent them and to help families in crises. If this fragmented approach was applied to health care, we would immunize only a fraction of our population and then treat only a fraction of the individuals who became infected. The result would be pandemics of diseases as we now see with our educational failures, endemic crime and welfare dependency.

We no longer can afford to ignore the causes of our intergenerational poverty, crime and welfare dependency. United Nations statistician Howard Friedman has carefully documented the declining international status of the United States in his book *The Measure of a Nation: How to Regain America's Competitive Edge and Boost Our Global Standing*. He bases this on the following facts:

- Americans have the lowest life expectancy among all competitor nations.

- Americans are at least two times more likely to be murdered and four times more likely to be incarcerated than any other competitor country.

- The United States shows the greatest disparity between rich and poor among all competitor nations.

While our nation focuses on current unemployment, the soaring national debt and terrorism, the ailments that infect our society are being ignored. Especially dangerous is the decline in thriving families that threatens the prosperity and security of our nation. This decline in family wellbeing deprives us of parents who are able to develop the characters and wellbeing of our young people…our nation's greatest natural resource.

This book is the story of my gradual recognition as a psychiatrist and volunteer lobbyist with state and federal governments that we live in a juvenile ageist society. We readily deplore prejudice based on age against the elderly while we ignore prejudice based on age against our even more helpless and unrepresented children. We deprive millions of young people of opportunities to become productive citizens as we say we are devoted to them. We can overcome this hidden discrimination by first accepting its existence then by ensuring that all newborn babies have competent parents.

The vast majority of struggling families do not receive the help they need. Fortunately, the coordinated interdisciplinary approach I began using in the 1970s is now being applied in many communities throughout our nation. When mental health, social work, educational, law enforcement and court professionals work together as a team—like the health care system tries to do—even the most difficult family problems can be resolved.

Most importantly, with a few notable exceptions like James Heckman and Hazel Henderson, economists have not considered the role parenthood plays in our nation's economy. Competent parents who raise one child to become a productive citizen contribute $1.4 million to our economy in earnings and taxes during that child's adulthood. Incompetent parents who abuse and neglect their kids cost our economy $2.8 million per child in lost earnings and taxes and in the costs of special education, crime, and welfare dependency. (Appendix 1) An estimated 23% of our state and 45% of our county expenditures are devoted to struggling families. (Appendix 2)

Fully one-third of our children and adolescents are not doing well. Over 11 million have been damaged by neglect and/or abuse. School failures, addictions, crime and welfare dependency are largely preventable if we simply would do one thing: ensure that all newborns have competent parents. My central theme is a fact that unfortunately is not reflected in popular beliefs:

The unpaid career of parenthood is more important for the health of our nation's economy than paid jobs.

This theme is based on the following indisputable facts:

1) Without parenthood, we won't have citizens;
2) Without competent parents, we won't have competent citizens and workers; and
3) Without competent citizens and workers, our economy won't prosper.

Incredibly, we presume that anyone who conceives a child is capable of raising that child. We do little to prepare individuals for the most important role in our society. We have no standards or guidelines for parenthood except for people who want to adopt children...and pets. We equate the human right to procreate with parental rights. What's more, our society's emphasis on materialism and individualism distracts parents from creating and sustaining the attachment bonds that are the very foundation of every child's emotional, cognitive, social and moral development.

Our society clings to the illusion that we treasure our children and support parents...especially by adulating parents who sacrifice in order to give their children every material advantage. In reality, a strong undercurrent undermines parenthood. Social policies, media advertising, the internet and societal norms make the already challenging job of being a competent parent more difficult. This reflects a deeply ingrained prejudice against individual children and childhood: *juvenile ageism*. This hidden prejudice, which is every bit as virulent as racism and sexism, makes it possible to ignore the wellbeing of our nation's children and families.

If we really care about our children, asks David Lawrence, former publisher of the *Miami Herald,* how is it that so many are treated so badly? Do we just not care? Are we not making the case coherently? Do we think we don't have the power to make people listen? Is it a lack of leadership? Lawrence points to all of these reasons but if forced to select one, it would be the lack of leadership.

The intent of this book is to inspire leadership to ensure that all newborn babies have their most basic and essential requirement for an opportunity to succeed in life: competent parents. We can do this by the small, but powerful, step of implementing a meaningful Parenthood Pledge.

Chapter One

Why Thriving Families are Essential
for Our Nation's Prosperity

*Each of our children represents either a potential addition
to the productive capacity and the enlightened citizenship of
the nation, or, if allowed to suffer from neglect, a potential
addition to the destructive forces of the community.*

THEODORE ROOSEVELT
SPECIAL MESSAGE TO CONGRESS, 1909

*Let's do our part to make sure none of our children
start the race of life already behind.*

BARACK OBAMA
STATE OF THE UNION ADDRESS, 2013

Nick Johnson was a handsome, cocky thirteen-year-old with long, black hair that fell across his forehead. His family was referred to our psychiatric clinic in 1970 by a juvenile court judge because he had run away, shoplifted and was prone to aggressive outbursts.

Nick was the oldest of four children, each of whom had behavior and learning problems. His mother, Shirley, was seventeen when he was born.

His eighteen-year-old father, Mike, was a chronic alcoholic and married Shirley during her first pregnancy. The pair separated and reunited three times before finally divorcing in the context of domestic violence.

On several occasions Mike attacked Nick. Once Mike threatened to kill Nick when he tried to protect his mother. Since Nick was four-years-old, Shirley had repeatedly asked for help. She'd received battered women's assistance, crisis intervention and respite services for the children.

Our psychiatric evaluation revealed that Shirley had a borderline personality disorder. Nick had a conduct disorder. His eight-year-old brother Tyler and his four-year-old brother Jess had attention deficit disorders. His ten-year-old sister Marlene had social phobias. Each child had been previously seen in medical and psychiatric clinics. Whenever clinicians had recommended family therapy, Shirley had not followed through.

Our recommendation was that the judge order family therapy. That was done and family sessions began. It became evident that Shirley encouraged her children's misbehavior by sometimes giving in to them and other times screaming at them. She blamed her children's problems on Mike and her temper on the children. When her role in the children's problems was addressed, she asked for her own therapist in another clinic.

Shortly thereafter, Nick ran away in a stolen car. Shirley claimed that Nick had become worse since family therapy had started and asked for a change in the court-ordered treatment. In spite of our explanation that the increased discord was related to the anxiety Shirley felt from facing her own issues, her request was granted. She returned to a pattern of sporadic individual treatment for each child with crisis intervention services.

One year later Nick was arrested for assault and battery. The seriousness of his offense landed him in a state correctional school. Tyler was placed in a special education program due to his mounting behavioral problems and failing academic performance. When Jess was screened for kindergarten, he needed speech and language therapy. By then Shirley was living with another alcoholic man. She continued to periodically use respite care.

Two years later, after Nick was released from the state correctional school, he shot and killed a store clerk. He was remanded to adult court and received a life sentence. A combination of medications was used to treat Tyler's increasing aggression. Jess didn't respond well to medication and was moved to a different special education program. Although Marlene was no longer mute with adults and earned passing grades, she remained socially isolated

What Went Wrong?

The Johnson family might be thought of as underserved or mismanaged by the professionals who tried to care for them. But they lived in a city with abundant resources and sophisticated professionals. Still these services didn't improve her children's problems that worsened.

According to the individual mission statements of each program, the services were used appropriately. Each crisis was managed by responding to Shirley's requests and providing respite care. Medications were prescribed by physicians, and schools developed Individual Education Plans for each child. In the end, though, these services allowed Shirley to avoid facing her role in her children's problems. She created an unconnected set of professional services in which each of the children was viewed as having a disability and/or a behavioral problem.

This result still is common today. Manipulative parents can abuse services that focus on the products of their own psychopathology rather than on them. Their children who create problems for others are victims of their own parents' failures. The children are exploited by parents who blame their children for their own failings and who then seek and often receive relief for their own personal anxieties.

Shirley's scapegoating of her children was reinforced by services that dealt with the children as individuals outside of the context of their families. It was further reinforced by biological and cognitive explanations of their behaviors and disabilities. Shirley could claim that her children's personalities caused their problems and her distress. Although Nick did have predisposing temperamental characteristics, he was punished for behavioral patterns ingrained early in his life. His victimization was obscured as he became a perpetrator.

If the recommendations for family therapy had been followed and monitored, the outcome could have been quite different. Unfortunately, unconnected services allowed the mother to avoid personal pain, obtain financial benefits and maintain her image as a concerned and abused parent. The sacrifice of her children's development and lifelong potential was hidden beneath professional validation of their disabilities and behavior problems. The responsibility for their problems was shifted to the children as well as to biological factors.

This unintentional professional support of personal and social problems could be attributed to ignorance or misguidance. But whenever the opportunity to address the victimization of the children arose, professionals sided with a manipulative mother rather than advocate for her children. Professionals deferred to her manipulations and accepted viewing the children as the sources of her problems. Some professionals concentrated on how Shirley suffered through her husband's domestic abuse and were distracted from how she victimized her own children.

Over the years, members of this family—excluding the father—were seen by twelve therapists, six social workers, fourteen special education teachers, three speech therapists, six physicians, three crisis intervention teams, and a respite care service in addition to the criminal justice system. Even today millions of families like the Johnsons still are a drag on the productivity and prosperity of our society. Chapter Twelve describes Collaborative Systems of Care that have evolved over recent decades and that should be available to all of these families.

PARENTHOOD IS THE WELLSPRING OF OUR SOCIETY

Our nation's future depends upon parenthood, the wellspring of our society. Parenthood is the source of the human capital essential for our economic prosperity, for our national security and for protecting our non-human environment. The loss in human capital caused by incompetent parents undermines our economy.

Each child raised to become a productive citizen contributes $1.4 million to our economy. Each child damaged by parental abuse and neglect like Nick costs our economy $2.8 million.

The usual prescription for improving our economy is to improve schools by hiring skilled teachers and getting kids to work harder. That plan never mentions parents. It's as if schools have the greatest and only influence on children…never mind the families and neighborhoods in which they live. The implication is that good schools can make up for bad families and bad neighborhoods.

Ignoring parents and neighborhoods is egregious. Disadvantaged competent parents with failing public schools actively seek alternative schools, such as in the charter system. Ignoring the fact that good schools are successful because they have the active support of competent parents denigrates parenthood and reflects juvenile ageism, both of which will be dealt with in detail in later chapters. For now, the exclusive focus on schools ignores these harsh facts. Of our children:

- 1 in 3 live with single parents, most without a father.

- 1 in 4 experience divorce.

- 1 in 5 live in poverty.

- 3 million are referred to child protective services every year.

- 11 million children have been seriously damaged by abuse and/or neglect.

Responsibility Starts at Home

These figures might well create a sense of helplessness. No wonder it's easier to believe that good schools will solve our problems, especially when schools are politically attractive as targets and as solutions. But blaming schools or expecting them to rescue foundering children from incompetent parents ignores the unmotivated, disrespectful students they are trying to educate.

Of course, many schools must be improved. Among developed nations, the U.S. ranks 26th in public school effectiveness. Many of our public schools have rundown facilities and ineffective teachers. Since women can become doctors, lawyers, corporate executives and governors, the best and the brightest no longer enter teaching as the most accessible career. The result is that half of our current teachers graduated in the bottom rather than the top third of their high schools.

Finland and South Korea, countries that outperform the United States in education, have three fundamental differences: 1) parents who support their children's education; 2) teachers who are well-paid and respected; and 3) relatively homogeneous populations. Finland's approach to education is so strong that only one in ten applicants for teacher training programs is accepted.

Our public schools can do a better job. If we devote the necessary resources, American education can once more lead the world in the qualities that characterize its best potential: *learning how to learn* by problem solving, being creative, thinking for one's self and questioning authority. Educational reformers like Sal Khan are leading the way with videos and software that blend individualized and group learning in a way that captures students' interest and energy.

Still, the unpaid job of parenthood trumps paid jobs and schooling in its immediate and lasting economic impact. We can no longer drift with the illusion that our gross domestic product (GDP) measures society's well-being while our human natural capital erodes. According to the latest data from the Vassar College Index of Social Health for 1970 to 2009, as our GDP has risen, ten indicators have worsened:

- Child poverty

- Income inequality

- Child abuse and neglect

- Teenage suicide

- Unemployment

- Average wages

- Health insurance coverage

- Food stamp coverage

- Access to affordable housing

- Homelessness

As will be shown in Chapter Two, one-third of our children and adolescents aren't doing well in some aspect of their lives. And many aren't from economically disadvantaged families. Substantial parent-child bonding deficits plague our middle and upper income homes where high-powered jobs and financial debts divert time and energy away from family life.

Fed by consumerism and contradictory, often unscientific, advice about brain development, parents from all social classes are confused about their children's basic needs. They are misled into believing that toddlers should watch educational DVDs so they'll learn to read by the age of three. They're encouraged to have preschoolers compete on T-ball and soccer teams to get a head start in athletics and to "red shirt" their children by delaying their entry into kindergarten. Such wrongheaded advice omits the core needs for children just to be themselves and for their parents' time and affection. It also ignores their need for parents as positive role models of caring, moral and productive citizens.

Competent parents produce children with the drive and imagination that have made, and that can continue to make, this country great. Children become responsible adults when they internalize the values of responsible parents through limits that impart self-discipline. Children learn to be responsible for their own behavior when their parents acknowledge their own mistakes.

Parenthood has a number of benefits. It is a marker of adult status and social acceptance. It reproduces the family and connects generations. A child brings joy and new life experiences. Children are persons to love through a lifetime. Their accomplishments can reflect positively on parents.

At the same time, the costs of parenthood are significant. Monetary expenses increase and the loss of income is possible. Opportunity costs associated with career, leisure activities and free time are incurred. Psychological costs show when parents have less time for themselves, decreasing flexibility and mobility and increasing worries and concerns. There are even physical costs from the strain of childbearing, childbirth, breast feeding and lost sleep.

The U.S. Department of Agriculture estimates that it costs over $220,000 to raise one child over the course of seventeen years in a two-child, married-couple, middle-income family. For this reason alone, parenthood has enormous financial implications for our society that currently does not appreciate the enormous investment parents make in producing our citizens.

OUR VULNERABLE ECONOMY

Financial journalist Jeff Madrick shows how our financial sector has evolved for the worse over the last forty years. The most recent recession repeats a pattern of financial overreach and government bailout followed by prosperity on Wall Street. Instead of improving America's productivity by allocating capital according to its best use, Wall Street has diminished our nation's productivity by focusing on stock prices and compensation packages. This pattern began in the 1970s when inflation and unemployment soared simultaneously. In *The Great Divergence*, journalist Timothy Noah notes that the democratization of incomes that has been taken for granted in the United States has reversed.

Today young adults especially are suffering from a recession created by years of emphasizing consumption rather than moderation without planning for the future of our young citizens. They inherit ruinous state and federal debts because of excessive borrowing and technology-driven money management in the private and public sectors. Over the last decade our federal government cut taxes, added health care benefits and started two wars without raising revenues—all at a time when money should have been set aside for almost 50 million Boomers now entering retirement.

Over the past two decades, household debt skyrocketed. Many Americans leveraged their home mortgages to maintain their standard of living while actual wages fell. More than 15% of Americans now live in poverty. Child poverty exceeds 22%. The top 1% of our population owns 36% of all wealth. An American CEO's paycheck is 475 times larger than the average worker's.

Despite growth in productivity, American workers have not been compensated at the same rate. Many workers earn less today than they did forty years ago. In 1964, production and non-supervisory employees claimed real average weekly earnings of $313. In 2010, the real average was only $294. Alongside this shrinkage affordable credit, routine work, government jobs and entitlements are being taken away from the middle class. The "family wage" that used to provide enough for a single earner to support a family has disappeared.

The Gallup-Healthways Wellbeing Index, which has polled over 1,000 adults every day since 2008, reports that Americans feel worse about their jobs and work environments than ever before. People of all ages across income levels are unhappy with their supervisors, apathetic about their organizations and detached from their jobs. They lack a sense of progress in meaningful work.

Ironically, our vulnerability is rooted in our failure to grow or sustain the greatest economic engine the world had ever known—the American work force. In 2011, the Manufacturing Institute, the official policy and advocacy arm of staple industries, reported that one third of U.S. manufacturers cannot find qualified workers despite the recession.

McKinsey & Company, a nonpartisan American global research and consulting firm, estimated that if U.S. students had met the educational achievement levels of other nations between 1983 and 1998, America's GDP in 2008 could have been $1.3 trillion to $2.3 trillion higher. In 2009, 75% of seventeen- to twenty-two-years-old were deemed unfit to serve in uniform. The primary reasons included an inability to pass the basic qualification test for math, literacy and problem-solving; being overweight and physically unfit; or being mentally or emotionally unfit.

America's decline is not simply the result of policy failures and the failure to develop human capital. Our decline and China's rise reflects inevitable shifts in world power structures. If the current trend continues, China's economy will overtake the American economy by 2027. By 2050, it will be almost double that size. Then as now, economic interdependence will likely be the most significant motivation for collaboration.

We need to shift our economic model away from consumption and back to production; away from concentrating wealth in the hands of a few and instead linking it to the contribution people make to our society; away from entitlement to investing in our human infrastructure, skills and technology; and to creating a society that offers opportunities for everyone.

In *A National Strategic Narrative*, Wayne Porter and Mark Mykleby note that our greatest renewable and sustainable natural resources are our young people. Students from Boston to Beijing are hungry to discuss the ethical questions we confront every day. They will shape and execute the vision needed to face an uncertain future. Because our nation has been so fortunate, many of us have forgotten that rewards must be earned. There is no free ride. Fair competition and hard work bring realistic accomplishments.

We can no longer expect the ingenuity and labor of past generations to sustain our growth. We must embrace the reality that challenges come with opportunities and that retooling our competitiveness requires a commitment to and investment in the future. Most of all, it requires a citizenry with the capacity for productive teamwork and for advancing the common good.

THE KEY TO A PRODUCTIVE WORK FORCE

Secure attachment bonding during childhood is the key to a productive work force. Despite the middle and upper middle class having adopted attachment bonding as a mantra, most parents today do not comprehend, nor are they encouraged to absorb, its implications. Attachment bonding refers to the connection between a parent and child forged in a child's early years. Most of a child's emotional, social, cognitive and moral development depends on this connection.

The science of attachment bonding is one of the great contributions of psychological research to Western civilization. Behavioral scientists have shown that a secure parental attachment bond increases a child's sense of security, self-respect and self-control. The impact of that attachment reaches far beyond children's emotions. The quality of that first human bond also affects how well they'll learn in school as well as their ability to get along with others.

The development of self-discipline and collaborative skills in childhood is the essential prerequisite for an adult's ability to work productively in teams; to become a compassionate and involved citizen; and to become a competent parent. An insecure attachment bond with parents produces school-aged children and adults who lack self-discipline and consideration for others. Such individuals often are self-centered, impulsive and exploitative. They did not learn to trust others starting with their parents. By the time these insecurely attached children get to school, much of their potential has already been lost. They become adults who lack the emotional intelligence to form positive relationships. They have difficulty collaborating within their families and in their workplaces. They continue the cycle of unstable family bonds that further weakens our society.

For all these reasons, *the quality of a child's attachment bonding is more vital to our workplace productivity and to our collective future than the quality of a child's education.*

Throughout this book, individual traits of children who either possess or lack secure parental bonding are linked with the same traits in our larger society. I do this in order to cast a spotlight on the crucial choice confronting America today. We can either continue down the road of individualism and materialism or strive for an integrative society that prizes moral character, teamwork and a higher quality of life for all.

Such a society would provide more security in an increasingly insecure world while helping us retain our position as global leaders. Recognizing a newborn's right to competent parents while enacting policies and providing resources to make that right a reality are the necessary first steps in this paradigm shift. If we did so, we would become a nation in which every person truly has an opportunity to succeed.

The Developmental Stages of Parenthood

This book is not just about child development. It also is about the developmental stages of parenthood…an unfortunately neglected topic. Fully realized, these stages help adults become better parents and enhance personal fulfillment. Each stage develops increasingly complex emotional, social, cognitive and moral skills.

As with other life stages, most parents successfully raise their children without consciously recognizing these developmental phases. They enhance their coping skills, altruism and self-respect as they work through their unresolved developmental issues triggered by the act of parenting. Individuals who successfully master these challenges achieve new levels of psychological and emotional maturity…as do their children.

Many parents need help in learning how to grow alongside their children. Some need education and clinical treatment to function competently. A comparatively small percentage (4%), nevertheless a critically large number (6.6 million), is simply unable to function competently. Typically these parents are minors and dependent adults under the guardianship of others or of the state.

Considering today's scattered, weak family networks, it makes no sense that society fails to prepare new parents for the challenges of parenthood. It makes no sense that we have no minimum standards for assuming the legal and physical custody of a dependent human being—a newborn baby. Chapter Fourteen proposes a parenthood pledge that could only be made by persons who do not need the legal or physical custody or guardianship of others. By formally establishing parental rights as the legal and physical custody of a newborn, our society would demonstrate that we truly value children and parenthood. If we have the will, the means to do so are within our reach through Parenthood Planning Counseling.

The parent-child unit is inseparable. By devaluing parenthood and turning the job over to paid surrogates too early and for too long, we harm children and damage every institution we claim to honor: families, schools, communities and workplaces. To truly value parenthood and create and maintain the attachment bonds that are essential to a child's emotional health and character...as well as to our national prosperity and security... we need to change key public policies. Subsequent chapters outline these policy changes in detail.

LET'S FACE THE FACTS

Our society clings to the illusion that we treasure our children and support parents...especially by adulating parents who spend money so their children can have every material advantage. In reality, a strong undercurrent denigrates parenthood. This undercurrent is evident in social policies, media advertising, the internet and societal norms that make the already challenging job of parenthood more difficult.

We can no longer afford to ignore the glaring reality: incompetent parents cause social problems...competent parents prevent them. We must understand what children really need in order to flourish—which is not the same as being happy—and to become self-disciplined, productive, moral members of society. Finally, we must change public policies and economic priorities so that competent adults can fulfill the vital role of parenthood.

If we are to do these things, we must confront the belief that little can be done to strengthen parent-child bonds and families, a belief that hands responsibility for childrearing to institutions. Paid childcare, schools and professionals are expected to fill in when parents fail. Parents today are not held as accountable for their actions with their children as they are for their interactions with people outside their families. At the same time, children have become commodities in the marketplace.

Instead by investing in strengthening families and in our youth—our future scientists, doctors, statespersons, industrialists, farmers, inventors, educators, clergy, artists, service members and parents—we truly invest in our ability to successfully compete in and influence our global environment. By investing in promoting safety in our homes and neighborhoods we reduce the number of Nick Johnsons on our streets. Our first priority, then, should be developing a sustainable infrastructure of family resources so that parents can nurture America's youngest citizens.

Why aren't we doing this?

Shirley Johnson was thought of as a loving mother who needed professional support. Her children were treated for a variety of conditions and accommodated by schools, and her delinquent son was punished. Does this picture show that we live in a society devoted to the wellbeing of its young? Do we really do everything we can for our kids? Or do we live in a society that neglects its young? The rest of this book is devoted to answering these questions.

Chapter Two

Why Worry About Our Children?

*Never before have we subjected our children to the tyranny
of drugs and guns and things or taught them to look for
meaning outside rather than inside themselves, teaching them
in Dr. King's words "to judge success by the value of our
salaries or the size of our automobiles, rather than by the
quality of our service and relationship to humanity."*

MARIAN WRIGHT EDELMAN, 1995
CHILDREN'S DEFENSE FUND

Most of our children and adolescents are doing well, but at least one in three are not. We should not be misled by rhetoric. We should not take comfort in downward trends in social problems, such as adolescent pregnancies or drug usage. We should not be misled by the image of parents who center their lives around their offspring. Those parents provide unprecedented levels of lessons, sports, tutoring and camps while over 16 million children and adolescents live in poverty. Over 11 million have been damaged by neglect and/or abuse.

The growing gap in family wealth has created two sets of young people in the United States…those with educated, prosperous parents and those with less-educated, poor parents. As a result, most middle and upper class children and adolescents are thriving while most lower class children and adolescents are not. The backlash is evident in our unacceptable rates of child neglect and abuse, incarceration, homelessness and welfare dependency.

If you are one of the American adults who live in a home without children—a majority these days—you need to know that the wellbeing of our nation's children affects you. Dire consequences arise when those of us without children miss the connection between the wellbeing of our young and our wide-ranging social problems. We all must see the big picture... parents matter.

HIDDEN IN PLAIN SIGHT

The daily news reports the myriad of ways in which many of our young are failing to the detriment of our society and our economy. Why doesn't this attract more public attention? Why don't we make the connection between failing parents, failing children and a failing society?

Daniel Patrick Moynihan gave an answer. He pointed out that societies, like individuals, cover up troublesome social problems with "pain killers." He noted that the tolerance for deviant behavior increases over time. Deviancy is redefined in a way that excludes conduct we previously deplored. A prime example is homelessness. Intolerable in the United States thirty years ago, homelessness—even of families with children—s commonplace today.

Becoming numb to our social problems reflects our ability to adapt to stressful circumstances over which we believe we have no control. We become like the frog that fails to jump out of water heated so gradually that the frog allows itself to be cooked to death. We are being cooked by the plight of our young citizens and its impact on our society.

Measuring the wellbeing of our nation in economic terms like the Gross Domestic Product (GDP), the total value of goods and services produced, allows us to avoid facing our social problems. In fact, costs associated with crime, disasters and illness increase the GDP. Focusing only on the GDP blinds us to the health of our society and to the plight of our young people. We need better ways to accurately measure the wellbeing of our people.

The Index of Social Health compiled by the Institute for Innovation in Social Policy at Vassar College measures the wellbeing of real people. Sixteen social indicators are measured across all age groups. The index can be used to stimulate preventing rather than servicing our social and health problems.

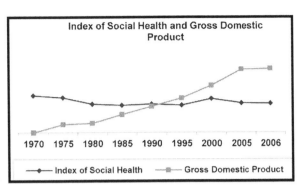

Intriguingly, as our GDP has risen, the Index of Social Health has declined. According to the latest data available (from 1970 to 2010), ten indicators have become worse:

- Child poverty

- Income inequality

- Child abuse

- Teenage suicide

- Unemployment

- Average wages

- Health insurance coverage

- Out-of-pocket health care costs for those sixty-five and older

- Food insecurity

- Access to affordable housing

- Homelessness

Six indicators have improved.

- Poverty among those sixty-five and older

- Infant mortality

- High school dropouts

- Teenage drug abuse

- Homicides

- Alcohol-related traffic deaths

The Annie E. Casey Foundation's *KIDS COUNT Data Book 2012* reported that four out of ten of their child wellbeing indicators have worsened.

- Children living below 100% of poverty, which increased by 1 million;

- The percentage of low birth-weight babies;

- The number of children living in families where no parent has full-time employment; and

- The number of children living in single-parent families.

Taken together, these conditions make the United States a leader among developed nations in signs of social distress. In his 1830s classic *Democracy in America,* Alexis de Tocqueville observed that individualism has its roots in England. From this comes de Tocqueville's prediction for our times: economically developed English-speaking countries will have the highest levels of social and developmental disarray.

The United States ranks 18th out of 21 Western countries in overall child wellbeing. Our children are clearly falling short intellectually. We rank 23rd in science, 17th in reading, and 31st in math achievement out of 32 Organization of Economic Cooperation and Development countries. These include Shanghai, China (1st in all), Finland (1st, 2nd and 6th), South Korea (6th, 2nd and 4th), Canada (8th, 6th and 10th), Germany (13th, 20th and 16th), and Poland (19th, 15th and 25th). Martin Carnoy, professor of education at Stanford University, found that, when socioeconomic status is taken into account, U.S. students fare much better than international test comparisons suggest. This underscores the socioeconomic inequality between students in the United States.

GROWING CHAOS FOR OUR YOUTH

These statistics shouldn't be surprising. Cornell University professor of human development Urie Bronfenbrenner, founder of the field of human ecology, called attention to the growing chaos in the lives of our children and adolescents twenty years ago. Since then we've seen:

- More children growing up in disadvantaged one-parent homes;

- Increasing conflict between the demands of employment and family life;

- Lack of positive adult role models;

- Erosion of neighborhood ties between families;

- Increasing divorce, step-families and one-parent families;

- A widening gap between the rich and the poor; and

- An increasing number of anti-social gangs.

Another way to evaluate our society is by identifying and measuring the assets our young people need to develop and reach their full potential. The Search Institute's Developmental Assets framework has two groups of twenty assets.

The *external assets* are the positive experiences (social capital) young people receive in their lives. These identify the roles played by families, schools, congregations, neighborhoods and youth organizations. The *internal assets* identify characteristics and behaviors (human capital) that reflect values, identities and social competencies that promote a commitment to learning. Having 31 of all of the 40 external and internal assets is the desirable level. In 2010 only 6% of our adolescents had achieved that level. The average young person has only 20 assets, and boys have fewer assets than girls. What's more, 37% of the young people surveyed reported being involved in 2 or more of the 10 dangerous patterns of high-risk behavior studied.

In 2006 prior to the current recession a Gallup survey developed by Child Trends and the Search Institute reported that only 31% of America's children had all or most of the basic supports needed for healthy development: 1) caring adults; 2) safe places and constructive use of time; 3) healthy start in life and healthy development; 4) effective education for marketable skills and lifelong learning; and 5) opportunities to learn how to help others.

Both affluent and disadvantaged young people show evidence of the "syndrome of alienation" described by Bronfenbrenner: 1) inattentiveness and misbehavior in school; 2) academic underachievement; 3) smoking and drinking; 4) sexual activity; 5) alcohol and substance abuse; 6) dropping out of school; and ultimately 7) violence, crime, homicide, suicide and welfare dependency.

Although genetic predisposition, pregnancy and birth complications, malnutrition, disabilities, poverty and racism contribute to children's vulnerability, whether or not they show the "syndrome of alienation" largely depends on how they were parented. When parents are consumed by alcoholism, drug addiction or mental disorders or when parents are preoccupied with personal interests or vocations and neglect and/or abuse their children, boys are prone to become criminals while girls are prone to become welfare dependent.

Physically or emotionally absent parents are the common denominator in the record numbers of young people with psychiatric disorders, daily medications, obesity and sexually transmitted diseases. These problems cross class boundaries. In *The Vulnerable Child: What Really Hurts America's Children and What We Can Do About It*, Richard Weissbourd concluded that the most serious threats to children—parental depression, a lack of meaningful opportunities, and social isolation—cut across class and race lines. An increasing number of affluent parents turn to therapeutic schools and programs like the 110 represented by the National Association of Therapeutic Schools and Programs.

POVERTY

In 2010, 22% of all people under the age of eighteen—over 16 million—lived in poverty...four times the rate in Scandinavia. Blacks were at 38%, American Indians 35%, Latinos 32%, Asians 14% and whites 13 percent. The statistics for children living in families where no parent has full-time employment were American Indian 51%, blacks 50%, Latinos 39%, Asians 32% and whites 27%. Harry J. Holzer, professor of public policy at Georgetown University, estimates that the economic costs associated with childhood poverty total $500 billion a year.

CRIME

Adolescents and young adults are victims of violent crime at the highest rates. In 2007, 20% of violent crimes were committed by juveniles. From 2004 to 2007, arrests of individuals under the age of eighteen for violent crime increased 4.5% while arrests for murder increased 19 percent. Between 1960 and 2009, juvenile court delinquency caseloads increased nearly 300 percent.

Homicide rates for U.S. males aged fifteen through twenty-four are more than four times those in other developed countries. Juvenile crime is rising especially quickly in the form of violence by girls in gangs. A decade ago, the ratio in arrests for assaults between boys and girls was ten to one. Now the ratio is four to one.

While violent crime has reached historic lows in cities like New York, Miami and Los Angeles, it is rising sharply in Milwaukee and other cities across the nation. Violent crime is expected to increase over the next decade as more violent felons are released from prison and the full impact of the recent recession is felt.

In the 1990s, homicides largely occurred in gang battles over drug turfs. Now they happen over petty disputes. In Milwaukee, a woman killed a friend during an argument over a silk dress. A man killed a neighbor whose ten-year-old son had mistakenly used his soap. Two men argued over a cell phone, pulled out their guns and killed a thirteen-year-old girl in the crossfire. Milwaukee Police Chief Nannette H. Hegerty called it "the rage thing. We're seeing a very angry population, and they don't go to fists anymore, they go right to guns."

The typical characteristics of adolescent crimes are demonstrated in shocking yet common examples. Five bored teenagers used Molotov cocktails to set fire to fourteen vehicles and one house. They took police on a tour of the arson spree and implicated themselves in three earlier house fires. Police said, "It was like show-and-tell."

Eighteen-year-old Sarah Rose Ludemann was stabbed to death by nineteen-year-old Rachel Marie Wade. According to a witness, Wade plunged a kitchen knife into Lundemann's heart. The two had been at odds over their on-again, off-again boyfriend, a nineteen-year-old who'd fathered a child with a third woman.

In Hillsborough County, Florida, sheriff's deputies arrested a fifteen-year-old and three fourteen-year-olds who violated a thirteen-year-old with a broom handle and a hockey stick in a locker room at Walker Middle School.

A dispute between two boys at a high school in an affluent suburb of Miami left one dead from a knife wound. A fourteen-year-old boy stabbed his best friend to death at a South Florida middle school. A handful of shootings and stabbings have occurred at schools in that area, although no one was killed.

In Chicago, more than 440 school-age children were shot in Chicago in 2012; 60 died. "I think people in Chicago have almost gotten numb to the statistics," said Dexter Voisin, a researcher at the University of Chicago. "For every kid who is murdered, about 100 kids witness a murder or are victims of nonfatal injuries, robberies, muggings and gang-related incidents."

BEHAVIOR PROBLEMS IN SCHOOLS

In a 2006 AP-AOL Learning Services Poll, two-thirds of the teachers surveyed said student discipline and lack of interest are major problems. School bus drivers must deal with disrespectful and unruly riders.

Even in the late 1990s, 47% of 3,500 kindergarten teachers surveyed said that at least half their students had problems following directions. Some of the issues were due to poor academic skills while others came from difficulties working in a group. When presented with the statement that an atmosphere of respect, trust and pride toward adults existed in their schools in a 2008 Pinellas County, Florida, survey, 37% of teachers disagreed. In Milwaukee public schools the number was 25 percent. Among students, it was 49 percent.

In the relatively prosperous Madison Metropolitan School District, 13% of the students and 42% of the teachers felt that parents were not helping them succeed. Among students, 22% felt they wouldn't get into trouble at home if they breeched school rules; 25% felt unsafe at school; 60% felt that their personal possessions were unsafe at school; 61% felt vulnerable to bullying; 54% felt vulnerable to sexual harassment; and 45% felt they couldn't talk with an adult at school about drugs, sex or suicidal comments made by other students.

Thirty years ago the disciplinary problems found in schools involved chewing gum, stepping out of line, tardiness and occasional fist fights. Today they include attacks on teachers, rape in the hallways, murder and suicide. From 1992 to 2006, over 400 murders occurred at lower-class urban schools and 33 shootings took place in middle-class schools. Many more deaths have been averted since then by early responses to warning signals. Children continue to shoot children but shootings no longer merit significant media attention. From 2006 to 2008:

- A seven-year-old boy shot a five-year-old three times. It was reported in the second section of the *St. Petersburg Times.*

- Seventeen-, sixteen- and thirteen-year-olds talked about how a fight would be fun then stabbed a thirty-four-year-old man to death.

- An eighteen-year-old Cape Cod Regional Technical High School student threatened to blow up the school with a pipe bomb he'd made.

- A fifteen-year-old boy in Clearwater, Florida, said he wanted to do something like the Columbine school shootings. In his room was a small arsenal together with videos of the shootings, executions and images of the president and vice president as targets.

- Two seventeen-year-old boys in Green Bay, Wisconsin, had weapons and bombs. They intended to repeat the Columbine shootings.

In February 2012, a school shooting in Chardon, Ohio, did receive national attention as did the December 2012 shooting in Newton, Connecticut.

Although there is no typical profile of school shooters, they consistently report that they had no adults with whom they could talk, including their own parents. A growing number of teenagers are uncontrollable and unreachable because they didn't form stable attachment bonds with their parents. Since they do not have effective consciences, they become drug addicts, thieves, rapists and murderers. Many were disadvantaged at birth by cocaine withdrawal or premature births and experienced frightening, insecure infancies. Their neglectful, often drug-using parents were unable to provide for their needs.

Bullying has reached unprecedented levels in our schools with suicide as a possible consequence. According to the Family and Work Institute, one-third of youth are bullied at least once a month, while others say six out of 10 American teens witness bullying at least once a day. Witnessing bullying can be harmful as it makes witnesses feel helpless or that they may be the next target. In a study by Fight Crime: Invest in Kids, nearly 60% of boys classified as bullies in grades six to nine were convicted of at least one crime by the age of 24, while 40% had three or more convictions.

THE ACHIEVEMENT GAP

Our nation faces a high school graduation challenge that will impede our nation's progress in the Twenty-First Century. According to the National Center for Educational Statistics, in 2010 78% of students across the country graduated within four years of starting high school. This figure included 93% Asian, 83% white, 71% Hispanic and 66% African-American. We must find a solution for what Professor Robert Balfanz of Johns Hopkins University calls our "dropout factories." At 12% of high schools, about 2,000 facilities, graduation is at best a 50/50 proposition. About 23% of young African-American male adult dropouts were incarcerated compared to a rate of 6% to 7% for Asians, Hispanics and whites. Female school dropouts are more than six times as likely to give birth and nearly nine times as likely to become single mothers as compared to peers who attended college.

In 1983, the National Commission on Excellence in Education warned that our educational system was failing. By 2001, the United States ranked 13th out of 15 developed countries in high school graduation rates. The Program for International Student Assessment found that fifteen-year-old

American students ranked 27th out of 39 developed countries in mathematical literacy and problem-solving skills. Some progress has been made by nine- and thirteen-year-olds; even there, the gains evaporate by the end of high school. Only 15% of the class of 2007 had a grade level that predicted success at the college level or higher.

According to the 2012 *Kids Count Report*, 68% of fourth graders were not proficient in reading, and 66% of eighth graders were not proficient in math. The percentage of high school graduates who enter college are 66% for Asians, 47% for whites, 40% for blacks and 32% for Latinos.

The percentage of students who graduate from community public college campuses within six years ranges from 17% to 58%. Twenty percent of college students completing four-year degrees, and 30% of students earning two-year degrees have only basic literacy and math skills. They are unable to estimate whether their car has enough gasoline to reach the next station or calculate the total cost for a variety of office supplies.

MENTAL HEALTH

In 2001, Surgeon General David Satcher released the *National Action Agenda for Children's Mental Health* in response to the crisis in mental health care for babies, children and adolescents. At that time, 10% of children and adolescents suffered from severe mental illnesses, yet only one in five received mental health services. In 2007, 20% of young people were diagnosed with a psychiatric disorder by the age of eighteen.

Emory University sociologist Corey Keyes' 2002 analysis of data from the *Child Development Supplement of the Panel Study of Income Dynamics* found that of fifteen- to eighteen-year-olds, only 40% were flourishing in mental health; 54% were moderately mentally healthy; and 6% were languishing. This age group also is characterized by:

- Increasing chronic mental and physical conditions related to the increasing number of premature babies.

- Substance abuse and eating disorders occurring at younger ages.

- Dramatic increases in asthma and obesity.

- Male rowdiness that masks emotional pain and often is diagnosed as attention deficit disorder.

One in five college students reports self-injurious behavior stemming from a history of abuse and adverse health conditions. More than two-thirds of adolescent students receive too little sleep, a condition the Centers for Disease Control's *2007 Youth Risk Behavior Survey* says increases behaviors that are harmful to a person's wellbeing.

The World Health Organization indicates that by the year 2020, child-hood psychiatric disorders will rise by over 50 percent. They will become one of the five most common causes of morbidity, mortality and disability among children. The lack of a unified infrastructure in the United States allows many of these children to fall through the cracks, as we saw with Nick Johnson in Chapter One. Too often, children whose mental health problems go unnoticed as well as those with recognized but untreated ail-ments end up in prison.

Our health care services do not sufficiently help adolescents develop healthy routines, behaviors and relationships they can carry into their adult lives. While most of our kids are doing reasonably well, most adolescents who need them don't have access to mental health and substance abuse ser-vices. Others engage in risky behaviors that jeopardize their current health and contribute to poor health in adulthood. Children and families suffer because of missed opportunities for prevention and early identification and because of fragmented treatment services.

CHILD MALTREATMENT

In 2009 the *National Survey of Children's Exposure to Violence* reported that more than 60% of children surveyed had been exposed to violence within the past year (i.e., as a witness to a violent act; by learning about a violent act against a family member, neighbor or close friend; or from a threat against their homes or schools).

According to the Annie E. Casey Foundation, 3 million children were referred to child welfare agencies in 2010. Of these, 675,000 were veri-fied to be victims of maltreatment. Almost five children died from ne-glect or abuse each day (1,760 in one year), 63% were neglected, 17% were physically abused, 9% were sexually abused and 7% were emotionally mal-treated. Seventy-nine percent of the perpetrators were parents. Other rela-tives accounted for 7% of the abusers, unmarried partners made up 4% and "other" filled in the remaining 10 percent. Most perpetrators were in their twenties or thirties. Nearly half of the perpetrators had emotional or behav-ioral problems yet only 24% received mental health care. The overall rates per 1,000 for ethnic groups were blacks 20, Pacific Islanders 18, American Indians 16, whites 11, and Latino 10.

A meta-analyis of North American studies by Rebecca Bolen and Maria Scannapieco published in *Social Service Review* revealed childhood sexual abuse in 25% of all girls and 16% of all boys. Men and women who experi-enced childhood sexual abuse attempt suicide at twice the rate of those re-porting no sexual abuse, have a 40% increased risk of marrying an alcoholic and are at a 45% increased risk of marital problems. Additional outcomes include substance abuse, running away from home, early menarche and early pregnancy.

The tendency of victims to remain silent about rape and incest protects abusers. The abuse might involve varying degrees of pleasure and guilt that complicate a victim's response. At the same time, some adolescents falsely allege abuse when parents frustrate their wishes. Even these allegations are cries for help for the family.

Centers for Disease Control and Prevention researchers found that per-sons who experienced considerable trauma during childhood died twenty years prematurely. Conservatively, child maltreatment directly costs our so-ciety over $104 billion a year.

ALCOHOL ABUSE, DRUG ABUSE, AND SMOKING

The *National Longitudinal Study of Adolescent Health* found that suburban high school students drink, smoke, use illegal drugs and engaged in delin-quent behavior as often or more than urban high school students.

- 63% of suburban and 57% of urban twelfth graders drink when away from family members.

- 40% of twelfth graders in both urban and suburban schools have used illegal drugs.

- 37% of suburban twelfth graders have smoked at least once a day compared to 30% of urban twelfth graders.

- Urban and suburban students are equally likely to fight and steal.

Half of all adolescents attended parties where drugs and alcohol were available. One-third attended a party where alcohol, marijuana, cocaine, ecstasy or prescription drugs were available while a parent was present.

More adolescents in the United States drink alcohol than smoke tobacco or marijuana. Underage drinking accounted for at least 16% of alcohol sales in 2001. Every year, 5,000 young people under the age of twenty-one die as a result of drinking. This number includes deaths from motor vehicle crashes, homicides, suicide and other injuries such as falls, burns and drowning.

According to the University of Michigan *Monitoring the Future National Survey* in 2011, 9% of eighth, 17% of tenth and 21% of twelfth graders reported having five or more alcoholic beverages in a row in the previous two weeks. Binge drinking by girls is increasing more rapidly than for boys. When compared with non-college age peers, college students have higher binge drinking percentages (41% vs. 34%). 9% in the 8th, 19% in the 10th and 25% of students in the 12th grades had used illegal drugs during the previous thirty days. The estimated abuse rates for illegal drugs other than marijuana were 3.4% in the eighth, 5.4 % in the 10th and 9% in the 12th grades.

In 2006 the Philadelphia School District acknowledged that the drug problem involving students from kindergarten through sixth grade was growing. Four bags of marijuana tumbled out when a ten-year-old took off his hat, and two more fell as he entered his classroom. Three fifth-graders took turns holding a bag of marijuana, and the student who brought the drug to school had $920 in his pocket. When a ten-year-old was searched for a knife after he threatened to stab another student, school officials found cocaine.

Adolescents use illicit drugs for recreation and prescription drugs for specific effects. Stimulants help them study, sedatives bring sleep and tranquilizers relieve stress. The 2010 *National Survey on Drug Use and Health Abuse* reported that the abuse of prescription drugs is highest among young adults ages 18 to 25, with 5.9% reporting nonmedical use in the past month. Among youth ages 12 to 17, 3% reported past-month nonmedical use of prescription medications. Nearly one-third believed there was nothing wrong with using prescription medicines once in a while; they also believed that prescription pain relievers aren't addictive.

About 90% of smokers begin before they turn twenty-one. The 2012 *Child Trends Data Bank* reported a positive trend. In 2011 2% of eighthgraders, 5% of tenth-graders and 10% of twelfth-graders reported smoking daily compared with 7%, 16% and 23% respectively in 1999. Most said they would like to quit but were unable to do so. Cigarette smoking during childhood and adolescence produces significant health problems including respiratory illnesses, diminished physical fitness and retarded lung growth.

OTHER RISKS

According to the Centers for Disease Control and Prevention, motor vehicle crashes are the leading cause of death among American teenagers. They killed 2,700 teenagers in 2010, a greater number than homicides and suicides. The accident rates among sixteen- to nineteen-year-olds is three times that of older drivers.

According to GASP, an educational campaign organized by parents of victims of the "choking game," seventeen-year-old Macklin Jensen died while participating in the game in which adolescents strangle themselves or have others push on their chests so they can feel lightheaded for a few seconds.

Each one of us carries at least 250 toxic chemicals in our bodies. The young are the most vulnerable to their damaging effects. The *Handbook of Pediatric Environmental Health* highlights lead, mercury, PCBs and pesticide poisoning as known hazards to children's health. Numerous studies confirm that even slightly elevated lead levels in the blood can cause learning and behavioral disorders, decreased IQ and hearing impairments. Many environmental chemicals mimic hormones that can disrupt developing immune, nervous and endocrine systems. The greatest vulnerability to toxic chemicals occurs during pregnancy.

All these chemical hazards are at their highest levels in the environments of disadvantaged, pregnant adolescents. Efforts to make manufacturers demonstrate that chemicals released into the environment are not hazardous to the health of children largely have been unsuccessful. This is in part because the thresholds for death from lead, PCB or mercury exposure are much higher than for altered cognitive and behavioral development. A disease like cancer also is more "real" than failing school performance.

ADOLESCENT SEXUALITY

According to the Centers for Disease Control and Prevention, one in four sexually active adolescent girls and boys (48% of black youth and 20% of white youth) contracts a sexually transmitted disease. These 4 million juveniles account for 25% of all cases. Of the some 900,000 adolescents who run away from home each year, over 6% test positive for the AIDS virus. Each year up to 64,000 adolescents spread AIDS.

Adolescent sexually transmitted disease rates are much higher in the United States than in most other developed countries. Rates are ten times higher for syphilis and gonorrhea, and two to five times higher for chlamydia. Although the age of sexual debut varies little across countries, American adolescents are the most likely to have multiple partners. The younger the sexual debut, the more likely health hazards become.

Adolescent childbirth is an international issue. Former President Bill Clinton wants to empower women to reduce birth rates because population growth is a major contributor to global warming. He calls for "slowing the population explosion in countries that can't take care of the people they have now."

Adolescent birth rates in the United States along with Bulgaria and Romania are the highest of developed nations. This is in part the result of the greater number of sexual partners among adolescents.

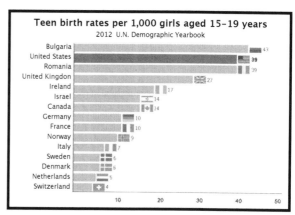

In 2009 the birth rate for girls ages ten to fourteen was 0.5/1,000, meaning that 5,029 gave birth. The birth rate for fifteen- to nineteen-year-olds was 39.1/1,000, meaning 420,600 gave birth. From 1990 to 2002, the pregnancy rate for fifteen- through nineteen-year-olds dropped from 111 to 76, a record low. This trend indicates an increased motivation to avoid pregnancies possibly influenced by reduced incentives to give birth through more restrictive access to welfare benefits in the Temporary Assistance for Needy Families program under the Personal Responsibility and Work Opportunity Act of 1996.

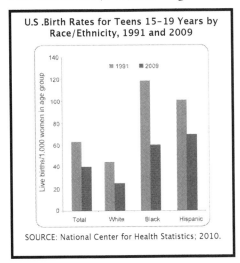

U.S. Birth Rates for Teens 15–19 Years by Race/Ethnicity, 1991 and 2009

SOURCE: National Center for Health Statistics; 2010.

Black and Latino girls are more than twice as likely as white girls to become pregnant at least once before the age of twenty. Still, over 2.5 million of our children and adolescents have been born to mothers under the age of eighteen. Almost a third of all sexually experienced adolescent girls have been pregnant. In one survey 22% of black, 19% of Latino and 10% of white boys reported having impregnated a girl. These figures are low since males might not always be informed about partners' miscarriages or terminations.

Adolescents ages fifteen through nineteen account for a third of all unwed mothers. Up to one-third of births to fifteen- to nineteen-year-olds result from desired pregnancies. Over one-third of these mothers become pregnant again within eighteen months. Most fail to return to school and become dependent on welfare. Less than 2% of mothers who have a baby before the age of 18 finish college by age 30. A substitute teacher in a New York high school made the following observation:

> I hear talk about becoming pregnant on purpose. I watch the girls who are pregnant become the center of attention, watch them feel important. I watch boys brag about the babies they've fathered as proof of their masculinity and see girls emotionally attach to boys like to the father they never had.

In 1960, adolescent childbearing occurred mostly in marriage with an employed husband. Now it is with unwed adolescents with limited prospects of marriage and economic security.

A National Campaign to Prevent Teen and Unplanned Pregnancy survey found that a majority of adolescent parents came from households that were not in poverty and that were not headed by single parents. However, a disproportionate share come from households with incomes either below or just above poverty levels as well as from households lacking one or both biological parents. The conception rate for boys is lower than the birth rate for girls because 39% of the fathers of children born to fifteen-year-olds, and 47% of the fathers of children born to sixteen-year-olds are older than 20.

Steeped in Social Toxins

In 1979, I found that 16% of our children had significant physical, developmental, mental, educational and social problems. Even more strikingly 37% of our children were thought to be at risk for maladjustment. The intervening years have borne out that forecast. Combining the following demographics indicates that at least one-third of our young people under the age of nineteen, some 24 million, have educational, health, mental health, behavioral or economic problems that impair the quality of their lives.

Indicators of Children and Youth Wellbeing	
Categories of Persons Under Nineteen	Percentage
Living in poverty[1]	22%
Did not graduate from high school on time[2]	22%
Have a diagnosed mental disorder[3]	20%
Substantiated victims of child maltreatment[4]	15%
In child welfare, juvenile justice, or homeless/runaway systems (ages 12 to 19)[5]	23%
Fourth graders not proficient in reading[1] Eighth-graders not proficient in math[1]	68% 66%
Twelfth-graders who:　　smoke once a day[6] 　　　　　　　　　binge drink[7] 　　　　　　　　　use illegal drugs[8]	10% 22% 10%
Abuse medications (ages 15 to 19)[9]	20%
Sexually transmitted diseases (ages 15 to 19)[10]	13%

Indicators of Children and Youth Wellbeing	
Rated as not flourishing in mental health (ages 15 to 19)[11]	60%
No parent has full-time employment (2010)[1]	33%
Children who are or have lived in one-parent homes[12]	50%
Personal assets:[13]	
positive self-esteem	52%
integrity	71%
achievement motivation	71%
delay gratification	50%
positive peer influence	68%

1) KIDSCOUNT 2012. New York: Annie E. Casey Foundation; 2) National Center for Education Statistics (2013) Class of 2010. Washington, DC: Government Printing Office. 3) Keyes, C.L.M. (2006) Mental Health in Adolescence. American Journal of Orthopsychiatry 76 (3): 385-402; 4) Administration on Children, Youth, and Families (2009) Child Maltreatment 2009. Washington, DC: Government Printing Office; 5) Perper, K. & Manlove, J. (2009) Vulnerable Youth: A Closer Look at Reproductive Outcomes. Putting What Works to Work September. Washington, DC: Child Trends. 6) 2012 Child Trends Data Bank; 7) Eaton D.K., Kann L, Kinchen S.A., et al. (2012) Youth Risk Behavior Surveillance—United States, 2011. CDC Morbity Mortality Surveillance Summary 61(SS-04):1–162; 8) Substance Abuse and Mental Health Services Administration (2012) Results from the 2011 National Survey on Drug Use and Health: Summary of National Findings, NSDUH Series H-44, HHS Publication No. (SMA) 12-4713; 9) Office of Applied Studies (2008) The NSDUH Report: Misuse of Over-the-Counter Cough and Cold Medications among Persons Aged 12-25. Rockville, MD: SAMHS. 10) Weinstock, H., et al. (2004) Sexually Transmitted Diseases among American Youth. Perspectives on Sexual & Reproductive Health 36: 6-10. 11) Keyes, C.L.M. (2006) Mental Health in Adolescence. American Journal of Orthopsychiatry 76 (3): 395-402. 12) Gottlieb, L. (2005) The XY Files. The Atlantic 296 (2): 141-150. 13) Benson, P.L., Scales, P. C. Roehlkepartain, E.C & Leffert, N. (2011) A Fragile Foundation: The State of Developmental Assets among American Youth. Minneapolis, MN: Search Institute.

James Garbarino, professor of psychology at Loyola University-Chicago, stands with Urie Bronfenbrenner in indicting our *socially toxic environment* that has created a larger number of children with serious problems today than was seen in the 1950s and 1960s. "Social contaminants" include exposure to violence, economic pressure, disrupted family relationships and behaviors stemming from depression, paranoia, bullying and alienation.

These social contaminants demoralize families and communities. The American Academy of Pediatrics confirmed this conclusion in its 2012 Policy Statement *Early Childhood Adversity, Toxic Stress, and the Role of the Pediatrician: Translating Developmental Science into Lifelong Health.* The Academy develops innovative strategies to reduce the effects of toxic stress in young children as well as negative effects on development and health across the entire life span.

William Julius Wilson, professor of sociology at Harvard University, points out that both societal and cultural impediments keep poor blacks from escaping poverty. Three generations of black ghetto dwellers have relied on sporadic work and welfare. Isolated in their urban neighborhoods, they have almost no contact with mainstream American society or the normal job market. As a result, they have distinctive and often dysfunctional social norms. A work ethic, investment in the future and deferred gratifica-tion make no sense when legitimate employment at a living wage doesn't exist and crime is both an everyday hazard and temptation. Men unable to support their families abandon them; women resign themselves to single motherhood and the status and benefits it accords; and children suffer from broken homes and antisocial examples set by peers and adults. This dys-functional behavior reinforces negative racial stereotypes, making it all the more difficult for poor blacks to find decent jobs.

We cannot expect our children to prosper when our society doesn't model and even undermines character development. The good life is por-trayed as having power, pleasure and possessions...gained by any means as described by Benjamin Barber in *Consumed: How Markets Corrupt Children, Infantilize Adults, and Swallow Citizens Whole*. Little emphasis is placed on the strength of character needed to control our impulses, to tolerate frustration and to postpone gratification—all essential for life in a civilized society. Children are not born with these qualities. They learn them from adults. They learn them most indelibly from competent parents supported by a social environment that supports families.

The child psychiatrist Harold Kopelwicz described "affluenza" as an illness contracted when people measure their worth with material goods. Children with this illness lack resilience. They have little patience or prob-lem-solving abilities; they don't understand cause and effect; and they lack independence in following through on tasks.

THE WAY IT IS

The growing discrepancy in family wealth has created two sets of young people: those with educated, thriving parents and those with less-educat-ed, poor parents. Only 31% of our children have all of the five basic sup-ports thought to be needed for optimal healthy development. One-third have significant educational, health, mental health or behavioral problems. Disruptive behavior in many schools necessitates the presence of police.

An increasing cohort of children is growing up uncontrollable and un-reachable because they did not form secure attachment bonds during early life. They do not have functioning consciences. As our physical and social environments become more toxic, our young show the effects first as well as the most.

Our society appears to need delinquents and criminals to act out the hidden impulses we gratify through violent, sexually stimulating media. We then subject offenders to indignant censure. In this sense, the "badness" of delinquents and criminals gratifies our own impulses. By punishing others, we can avoid facing our own "badness."

We need to strengthen struggling families in order to prevent antisocial behavior. Instead we expect schools and governmental agencies to correct our social problems, as if parents have nothing to do with the outcomes of their children's lives.

We can and must remove the barriers to developing a responsible, productive citizenry by helping the families of over 16 million young people find pathways out of poverty. We also must address the needs of over 11 million children and youth who have been damaged by neglect or abuse. When we elevate the bar of tolerable deviant behavior, we clearly denigrate our youngest citizens and their parents.

Chapter Three

The Denigration of Parenthood

The proper officers will take the offspring of the good parents to the pen or fold, and there will deposit them with certain nurses who dwell in a separate quarter; but the offspring of the inferior, or of the better when they chance to be deformed, will be put away in some mysterious, unknown place, as they should be.

They will provide for their nurture, and will bring the mothers to the fold when they are full of milk, taking the greatest possible care that no mother recognizes her own child...Care will also be taken that the process of suckling shall not be protracted too long; and the mothers will have no getting up at night or other trouble, but will hand all this sort of thing to the nurses and attendants.

PLATO
THE REPUBLIC

Plato's perfect republic was one in which children would be raised more efficiently by the state than by parents. Then adults would be free to pursue their own interests. Plato's Republic had parents without parenthood. Israeli Zionists in the early Twentieth Century thought the burden of childrearing and homemaking was the root cause of gender inequality. They emulated Plato's Utopian form of childrearing in their communes and tried to eliminate parenthood.

Zionist kibbutzim replaced marriage with cohabitation. A couple shared sleeping quarters but retained separate names and identities. Children were reared in community-run children's houses. Adults thought of kibbutz children as "joint social property" and were discouraged from developing close relationships with their offspring. Boys and girls were encouraged to think of the kibbutz itself as their parent. Thus freed from the domestic yoke, women engaged in productive work alongside men. Feminine clothes, cosmetics, jewelry and hairstyles were rejected. In order to be equals, women had to look like men as well.

Similarly, royalty and the wealthy have always hired others to care for their children. This motif of delegating parenting now permeates our own nation. The marketplace values only paid work, although it is encountering resistance from those who prize close relationships with their children. This resistance by parents led ultimately to abolishing the separation of parents and children in kibbutzim. Today kibbutzim support parenthood with parental leave, work adjustments to accommodate parenting tasks and family living. The society that once attempted to abolish parenthood became a strong advocate of parenthood.

A SNAPSHOT OF AMERICAN PARENTHOOD

Parenthood generally is not accorded a high value in the United States. Having a baby is a status symbol…caring for one is not. Unlike other Western nations, the United States does not recognize the economic value of parenthood. Many parents are diverted from childrearing to paid employment either by choice or by necessity in welfare-to-work programs. Childcare is regarded as a marketable educational function rather than a fulfilling developmental experience for adults and children.

In her book *The Outsourced Self*, professor emeritus of sociology at the University of California-Berkeley, Arlie Russell Hochschild points out that the rise of feminism coincided with a drastic lengthening of work hours and a steep decline in job security. In the United States those stressors have not been alleviated by social supports like paid family leave and universal childcare, at least not in comparison with most other Western nations. As a result too many family and community bonds are strained by anxious, overworked couples; too many family functions have been subcontracted; and too many children perceive themselves as burdens.

Our nation has viewed childrearing as a private matter unless it is terminated by death or abandonment or when parents damage their children by neglect or abuse. Otherwise our society has limited its role to public education. In many circles, parenthood has come to be regarded as an optional accessory rather than as a developmental stage in the life cycles of men and women. In his book *What to Expect When No One's Expecting,* Jonathan V. Last writes that pets now outnumber children 4 to 1 in the United States.

The disparagement of parenthood is felt particularly strongly by adults who place parenthood above employment away from home during their children's early lives. The term "working" women and men refers to people who are employed away from home and implies that homemaking is not work or at least is less important than paid work.

What's more, the economic benefit of the family has largely disappeared. Children are no longer economic assets and are costly liabilities instead. The growth of Social Security, Medicare and pensions has reduced the need for the support of one's offspring in old age. More young workers are needed to support these programs for older citizens. Parents must produce the vital human natural capital that keeps our economic system going even as greater life options make nurturing the next generation less attractive. More adults are opting to not have children. Most importantly, later chapters of this book will show how public policies and workplaces stack the odds against those who choose to raise our nation's children.

One result in all advanced nations has been a dramatic fall in birthrates—often to well below replacement rates—and rapidly aging populations. At the same time, the state of family life has become deeply problematic. High rates of divorce, out-of-wedlock births and increasing downward mobility of parents abound. Marriage is being replaced by cohabitation. Virtually unheard of thirty years ago, homeless families are commonplace today.

In addition to creating the childcare industry as a capitalistic supplement to parenthood, our society is imbued with materialistic beliefs that encourage parents to seek alternatives to caring for their children. One widely held belief is that both parents should be employed away from home on a full-time basis in order to generate enough income to pay for high quality childcare along with luxury goods and services.

Another belief is that commercially fostered trends of consumption reflect success and sophistication. Parents are attracted to professional expertise and novel technologies that free them from menial chores like childrearing. When you can pay someone else to do a tedious job better, why do it yourself? Even when childrearing appeals to adults, the lack of social support for a task regarded as "caretaking" or "caregiving" rather than as an interactive growth process for children and adults undermines its value.

Because children are the *raison d'être* of parenthood, anything that undermines parenthood detracts from children's developmental needs. Both obvious and subtle disparagement of parenthood adversely affects children.

PARENTHOOD IN SECOND PLACE

A civilization's growing complexity brings competition among interests and activities. Childrearing is increasingly delegated to institutions, such as schools and childcare facilities. Rather than being the primary activity of adults, parenthood often is relegated to second place by necessity and by choice.

Because it is unpaid, parenthood doesn't have direct economic value while paying others to care for children does. Parents therefore seem to be more useful to society in the work force where productivity can be valued in monetary terms. Hiring non-parents to care for children also creates jobs that increase the GDP. Still, childcare's financial value is comparatively low and most is of poor quality.

Only 1 in 3 households in the United States has a child under the age of eighteen. A Gallup survey that found that employment away from home makes it easier for women to lead personally satisfying lives. It also makes raising children and maintaining a successful marriage more difficult when men do not value parenting and homemaking. Marriage and parenthood have been separated. Parenthood even seems to have become an obstacle to a successful marriage for some parents.

Jennifer Westfeldt's movie *Friends with Kids* questions why people need to experience romance with the same partner with whom they raise children. "Best intentions aside," Westfield says in a *New York Times* article, "having kids always changes your friendship...in a way that I think is painful for both of you."

As with other civilizations, successive generations of Americans have been concerned about the deterioration of families as they adapt to new social conditions. In recent decades, consumerism has particularly affected family life. Following World War II, parents felt a strong commitment to give their children more material things than they had during their childhoods in the Great Depression. Overindulged children lost respect for parents and authority. The Vietnam War intensified the disillusionment of the young in their elders. Later decades were dominated by the Cold War and fear of nuclear attacks.

Now an anti-authority, postmodern philosophy permeates our society with its emphasis on self-assertive individualism. An ethos of avoiding discomfort and frustration has risen to the top. Both young and old adults can choose options that are "best for me." The pursuit of perfection further intensifies this ethos.

Henry Giroux, professor of cultural studies at McMaster University, describes the growing commercialization of our everyday lives, the corporatization of education, the dismantling of welfare, the securitizing of public spaces and the privatizing of public services. This trend has made it more difficult to develop family-friendly social policies that support parenthood.

PARENTHOOD IS NOT SEEN AS A CAREER

Most importantly, our society doesn't recognize parenthood as a career. It doesn't formally acknowledge that childrearing is skilled, hands-on work in which parents and children bond and grow together. It automatically awards full parental rights to any genetic parent regardless of age or ability until the child is damaged by the parent's neglect or abuse and parental rights are terminated by a court.

Nonetheless, parenthood *is* a lifelong career. Like any career, parenthood has its frustrations and rewards. Unlike any other career, it's based on affectionate attachment bonds. For most parents, parenthood is just as important as a paid career. This is especially evident during a person's later years. Louis Terman's Stanford study of eminent women and men found that, as they looked back on their lives, they valued family relationships over their professional careers.

We need to face the implications of parenthood as a lifelong career. Family life is changing rapidly in the face of increasing maternal employment, father absence and cultural diversity. Many parents need more than one income to make ends meet. In some families parent-child roles are reversed. At the same time, children are being treated as commodities by reimbursed systems that serve children. All of this takes place alongside increasing ambivalence about committed relationships and questions about who is the parent of a child conceived through IVF technologies.

Having "a parent" in itself means nothing to babies, children and adolescents. Anyone past puberty can be a parent...a mother or a father, but to enter parenthood is to have a career with a lifelong commitment to a daughter or son. Parenthood means everything to babies, children and adolescents. They need competent parents who can handle its responsibilities. Unfortunately, our society does not distinguish between merely being a mother or a father and motherhood and fatherhood. Consequently, it fails to ensure that our children have competent parents.

The extent to which parenthood can be demeaned inadvertently by child development professionals showed up in an article in *Zero to Three*, a professional journal devoted to early childhood, that listed "the needs of infants." On the list is *Infants need a special someone*. The word *parent* was replaced by *special someone*.

Contemporary ideas about childrearing place intense demands on parents and emphasize talented and independent children. Annette Lareau, a professor of sociology at the University of Maryland, notes that many upper-middle-class parents provide learning experiences for their children at an exhausting pace. In contrast lower-middle-class parents seem to believe that adulthood will come soon enough and that children should be left alone to create their own play. These children seem more relaxed and vibrant, and appear to enjoy more intimate contact with their extended families. Lareau commented:

> Whining, which was pervasive in middle-class homes, was rare in working-class homes. Middle-class adolescents feel en-

titled to individual treatment... Working-class adolescents feel constrained....

The rewards of parenthood are easily obscured for contemporary parents who have not discovered the satisfactions and pleasures of parenthood. Instead, they try to "have it all now" for themselves and their children.

Plato's idea of raising children away from their parents was not realized in ancient Greece. It failed in all subsequent childrearing experiments from the Israeli kibbutzim to the People's Republic of China. Even the wealthy who delegate childrearing often do not have rewarding family relationships. Still Plato's ideal is taking hold in the United States.

What's more our *society* doesn't formally articulate parenthood standards except for adoptive and foster parents. However, our *culture* does hold expectations for people who give birth to a child. The differences between social and cultural values will be outlined in Chapter Ten. The vast majority of children are raised by parents who fulfill these cultural expectations by building and maintaining parent-child bonds, but an increasing number are not. Pediatrician T. Berry Brazelton and child psychiatrist Stanley Greenspan suggested in their book *The Irreducible Needs of Children* that this underlies the general fragility of relationships in our society. Adults who didn't have caring, intimate relationships with their parents find sustaining committed relationships, including with spouses and offspring, difficult.

Because committed relationships are vital to our society's integrity and prosperity, we must articulate our cultural expectations of parenthood, the source of committed relationships. Implicit cultural expectations include a child's moral right to competent parents and the obligation to respect and cooperate with the child's parents. These cultural expectations have evolved into legal expectations codified in child abuse and neglect statutes. Because our society has not sufficiently valued parenthood, courts are increasingly involved in articulating our cultural expectations of parenthood.

THE ROLE OF COURTS IN DEFINING PARENTHOOD

Courts no longer hold that the human right to procreate also accords ownership of the child. When family matters are adjudicated, a variety of case and common law precedents define our expectations of parents based on our cultural values. Child abuse and neglect cases as well as divorce custody laws articulate these expectations.

In family courts, our cultural expectations of parenthood are to:

- Provide a home that legitimizes a child's identity in a community.

- Provide sufficient income for a child's clothing, shelter, education, health care and social and recreational activities.

- Provide the love, security and emotional support necessary for healthy development.

- Foster intellectual, social and moral development.

- Socialize the child by setting limits and encouraging civil behavior.

- Protect the child from physical, emotional and social harm.

- Maintain stable family interactions through communication, problem solving and responses to individual needs.

When we look at these expectations, we can see that we really do rely on parents to instill cultural values so that children will become responsible citizens. The need to explicitly recognize the essential role of parenthood and to support parents in childrearing becomes obvious. Parental incompetence at any point in a child's development can have unintended long-term consequences.

Defining Parental Competence

Because we all fall short of our ideal images, most parents doubt their competence. An initial reaction to any discussion of competence might be to define ourselves as incompetent. This overreaction creates a reluctance to deal with actual parental incompetence since doing so might involve judging all parents. In fact the vast majority of parents are competent.

Competent parents quite simply are committed to parenthood. Their behavior shows that they care about their children. They restrain themselves from harming them. They do not neglect or abuse their children in a legal sense. The definition of competent parents flows from our cultural expectations.

Competent parents are capable of assuming responsibility for their own lives, sacrificing some of their interests for their children, providing limits for their children's behavior and giving their children hope for the future.

They also have access to essential economic and educational resources, as will be elaborated in Chapter Ten. When necessary, society has an obligation to provide access to these resources. Just as there are dietary elements essential for physical growth, there are essential experiences for healthy personality growth. Children must learn to delay gratification, tolerate frustration, work productively and avoid harming others.

Young people acquire the values and skills essential for success through parents who possess these qualities. This does not mean that competent parents are social conformists who raise conforming children to become conforming adults. Our democratic republic depends as much upon parents who initiate changes. Our way of life depends upon diversity in opinions and lifestyles.

Most importantly, wealth does not ensure parental competence nor does poverty ensure parental incompetence. The empirical fact is that children raised by competent parents—including the poor and the physically handicapped—seldom become criminals and/or welfare dependent.

DEFINING PARENTAL INCOMPETENCE

A child's congenital handicaps and the lack of socioeconomic resources can make parenthood stressful for even the most competent adults. Incompetent parents, on the other hand, can't take responsibility for their own lives, much less for their children's. In legal terms, they are unfit. Most minimize or deny their incompetence. Their lack of skills can stem from immaturity or from personality, developmental, mental disorders or addictions. Even with support and treatment, many are unable to change soon enough to raise their own children.

Because incompetent parents have difficulty controlling their impulses, they are vulnerable to substance abuse and alcoholism. They are insensitive to the needs of others and are unreliable. They do not form stable attachment bonds with their children. They alternately neglect or overreact to their children's behavior with unpredictable and inconsistent cycles of indifference, idle threats and severe punishment. They have difficulty restraining themselves from harming their children.

Their children are confused when what happens to them bears little relationship to what they do. The parents' erratic behaviors result in inconsistent childrearing practices. As a result, the children of incompetent parents are insensitive to the needs of others and behave unpredictably. These children often become adults who don't control their impulses and who don't care how their behavior affects other people.

Incompetent parents can be detected without subtle techniques or tests. No unbiased, fully informed person would have any difficulty identifying them. A conservative look at child neglect and abuse reports reveals that about 4% of all parents are incompetent according to the above definition. This represents 8% of one-parent and 3% of two-parent homes. Although small in percentage, the number is significant...6.6 million. At least twice as many parents have not yet been adjudicated as abusive or neglectful.

Most people don't appreciate the impact this comparatively small number has on our society until the number of incompetent parents is multiplied by the number of children they produce. At least 11 million children have been seriously damaged by abuse and/or neglect. A larger number have had their lives impaired enough to create later adverse effects on their own offspring.

Neglect by incompetent parents is more harmful than physical abuse. It eliminates any opportunity to develop the social skills children need to become responsible human beings. In contrast, children who are abused but not neglected may be able to relate to other people. In that way they may be able to acquire the social skills needed for productive citizenship.

Damage caused by parental neglect is clear in developmentally delayed babies whose "failure to thrive" stems from the lack of attachment bonds. These babies don't feed properly and suffer severe enough delays in their physical, social and cognitive development to result in death.

The lack of prevention programs and the inability of child welfare services to therapeutically intervene with incompetent parents create situations our society no longer should tolerate. Two examples are provided below.

Mary

Mary was born to a sixteen-year-old alcoholic mother, who subsisted on Aid to the Families of Dependent Children and divorced twice before Mary was first brought to the attention of child welfare services at the age of 3 because of repeated allegations of parental neglect.

At the age of 9, Mary began to be sexually abused by an older brother. When she was 10, she was placed in a special class for the emotionally disturbed. When 13, she was brought to juvenile court because of alcohol and substance abuse and a year later placed in a county juvenile home. Her destructive behavior led to subsequent placement in two adolescent treatment centers.

When 15, Mary was sent to a state correctional facility and thereafter to a state mental hospital. After her release at 18, her first child was born. She subsequently was married and divorced three times. Her second child was born when she was 20. When her children were 2 and 4 years old, child welfare services intervened and placed the children in foster homes. Mary entered two alcohol and substance abuse treatment centers and did not complete treatment. She was arrested several times for drinking while driving, once in a near-fatal accident and later for the sale of illegal drugs. She sought and obtained the return of her children after serving three months in jail. Within two months Mary resumed drinking. Her children were placed again in foster care at the ages of 4 and 6. By that time their behavior problems necessitated psychiatric treatment.

When 25, Mary was sentenced to prison because of drug dealing. Her parental rights were finally terminated, and her children were placed in adoptive homes where they continued in psychiatric treatment and special education.

BethAnne

BethAnne was a 16-year-old bipolar child sexual abuse victim and crack-addicted prostitute with a pattern of threatening to kill her mental health worker. Child welfare services did not intervene until months after she left her baby with an ex-boyfriend's sister and an attempted murder charge was made against her.

We must recognize that not all people who conceive and give birth are competent parents. Identifying incompetent parents before they damage their children must be a high priority. Those who cannot be competent parents need relief from the responsibilities of parenthood through expeditious termination of their parental rights followed by adoption.

THE ROLES OF PARENTHOOD

Our society has a vital interest in ensuring that all children have competent parents. The two roles of parenthood, motherhood and fatherhood, should be thoroughly understood as part of this process.

Motherhood

A society's attitude toward motherhood is influenced by its attitude toward children. One consequence of juvenile ageism fully described in succeeding chapters is the devaluation of motherhood and of caring for the young. Welfare-to-work policies require mothers to take low-paying jobs even though maternal care during the first year is less costly than publicly funded childcare. Employment therefore is cast as more important than parenting. This is true even though parenting can reduce public expenditures and is in the interests of babies and mothers. More broadly, motherhood brings one of the most difficult decisions in a woman's life...stay at home, pursue a career or do both?

Often motherhood is seen as something that interferes with paid careers. Linda Hirshman, an emeritus professor of women's studies at Brandeis University, believes childrearing is not fulfilling for educated women. She is concerned about the current trend in which women are leaving the workforce to become full-time mothers.

Hirshman believes that the family with its repetitious, socially invisible tasks is a necessary social institution but that it does not allow women to flourish. Careers in business or government, after all, offer money and professional advancement as markers of success. Hirshman suggests that women devote their first few years after college to preparation for paid work. She wrote:

> Expensively educated mothers who stay at home are leading lesser lives. They bear the burden of work associated with lower social classes—housekeeping and childcare.

According to Leslie Bennetts, journalist and author, employed mothers are best for children. They exemplify resourcefulness and independence, and they demonstrate the virtue of engaging in work one loves. She suggests that women lose their humanity if they don't fulfill themselves through paid careers. In *The Conflict: How Modern Motherhood Undermines the Status of Women*, Elizabeth Badinter holds that an exalted view of motherhood can have the effect of controlling women and seeking to reconcile them to a lack of independence and frustrating their individual talents and ambitions. In contrast novelist Lisa Jackson said that empowering yourself doesn't have to mean rejecting motherhood or eliminating the nurturing or feminine aspects of who you are.

The demeaning of motherhood is also reflected in the dramatic changes in women's labor force patterns over the last twenty years. Many more mothers now work full or part time. The wage gap between men and women has narrowed but persists. According to the U.S. Census Bureau 2010 American Community Survey, the median annual wage for men was $45,672 and for women $35,553. Mothers earn about $1.50 an hour less than childless women. If they continue to be largely responsible for childrearing, mothers won't catch up. Since most women have children, this penalty continues to contribute to workplace inequality.

Still the Barnard College *Parenting Young Children Study* revealed that most mothers felt overwhelmed by the conflicting demands of raising children and employed careers but desired to do both well. When one had to give, most mothers were not willing to sacrifice the interests of their families.

In *Mass Career Customization*, Cathleen Benko and Ann Weisberg show how today's career path no longer means a straight march up the corporate ladder, but rather a combination of climbs, lateral moves and planned descents. According to Syliva Ann Hewlett of the Center for Work-Life Policy, 37% of all professional women leave employment at some point to rear children. Even more have flexible schedules, but only 40% of those who return to employment find full-time jobs. Even then, employment usually comes with a loss of earnings. This pattern has been exaggerated by the recession that began in 2008.

Fatherhood

The need to establish paternity for newborns underscores the vulnerability of fatherhood. In our society, almost 40% of all babies are born to unmarried mothers. To try to ensure that the babies obtain the support of both parents, federal policies encourage establishing paternity as soon as possible. This increases the likelihood that the baby will have a lasting relationship with the father and that child support will be paid. Different jurisdictions vary widely in rates of establishing paternity and in child support awards.

The form fatherhood takes also varies more widely than motherhood. Fathers are involved with their children in three ways:

- Living with their children.

- Visitation with their children.

- Responsibility for their children's support without a relationship.

A University of Michigan Institute of Social Research study revealed that at some point in their lives, half of all children don't live with their biological fathers. During a thirty-year period, 28% of the men who lived with the mothers at the time the children were born moved away. Men who cohabited with the mothers were more than twice as likely to live away from the children as married men. Forty-one percent of black fathers do not live with their children compared to 24% of white fathers.

The casual, unrealistic attitudes fathers can hold toward conceiving children is revealed by two young fathers:

> 20-year-old Anthony explained, "I'll use a condom with other girls, but not with my special girlfriend. Pregnancy, like, is for her. Still marriage is a big step. I might have a baby with her, but I haven't found Miss Right yet."

> 19-year-old Carmelo sold drugs so that his 2-year-old daughter could have "everything I wanted her to have. I felt like if I had a kid, it would settle me down." He took a GED course for a few months and spent less time hanging out with his friends. His girlfriend Shana thought getting pregnant would force Carmelo to stay around. She ended up on welfare after Carmelo left her.

CAN PARENTHOOD BE VALUED AGAIN IN THE UNITED STATES?

Social progressives look to Scandinavia as a model for child wellbeing. If the United States adopted Sweden or Norway's generous family benefits, they argue, we too could achieve low rates of child poverty, adolescent pregnancy and single parenthood. Social conservatives point to Sweden as a cautionary example of how generous social welfare policies weaken marriage and the family.

Neither side tells the whole story. Scandinavian cultures are child-friendly in the sense that children have basic rights. Their cultures stress an individual's responsibility to the common good of society compared to the American emphasis on individualism and on adult rights that tend to regard children as the property of their parents.

Child poverty barely exists in Sweden, and adolescent birthrates are very low. Few babies are in childcare because mothers have one year of paid family leave following childbirth. The Swedish marriage rate is one of the lowest in the world while divorce rates continue to rise. Sweden leads the Western nations in cohabitation. Breakups for these couples occur twice as frequently as in marriage.

The Swedish approach includes policies that many social conservatives would embrace such as strict limits on abortion, a six-month waiting period before divorce and a ban on IVF procedures for single women and anonymity for sperm donors. Still, the United States and Sweden are among the developed nations with the lowest percentage of children growing up with both genetic parents.

Despite these commonalities, the two societies are very different. Sweden is communitarian, comparatively ethnically homogeneous, socially cohesive and resolutely secular. America is individualistic, ethnically diverse and strongly religious. Though Scandinavian family policies might be models for a more child-friendly society, we cannot simply adopt their social policies and achieve the same results. The common good is a paramount value in their cultures... individualism is paramount in the United States.

WHERE DOES THIS LEAVE US?

In the United States, anyone past puberty can be a parent, but parenthood is a lifelong commitment to a son or a daughter. Only competent adults can handle its responsibilities. Work is defined in our capitalistic economy as a paid activity. Unpaid activities like childrearing are not regarded as work. This obscures the fact that childrearing has immense financial value. In the long run, parenthood is more important to our society than paid vocations. Although not recognized as such, parenthood is the career that benefits everyone whether it is in one-parent or two-parent homes.

Chapter Four

Marriage, Divorce and One Parent Homes

Does anyone understand that the jobless father often destroys himself, his family, and his community? Does anyone understand the frustration of the mother who knows that her children will need the best education possible, but she can't afford it and the national community won't help pay for it? Does anyone understand that the young men who make city streets dangerous and destroy themselves with drugs could have been proud, productive citizens? Does anyone understand that these problems can destroy this country?

RICHARD GORDON HATCHER
MAYOR, GARY, INDIANA, 1971

Marriage is the traditional arrangement for motherhood and fatherhood. For centuries, it's been regarded as the most important marker of adulthood and respectability and as a stabilizing influence on our society. It also has been a route to benefits like social security, health insurance and unemployment insurance.

In his book *The Marriage-Go-Round*, Andrew Cherlin notes that we have gone from a pattern of getting married young then having children and for the most part staying married to a bewildering set of alternatives. Choices include bearing children as a lone parent and perhaps marrying later; living with someone and having children without marrying; or following the conventional marriage-then-children script followed by a divorce and probably living with a new partner then maybe remarrying. Cherlin observes that we have gone from concerns over the consequences of conformity to "the tyranny of too many choices."

In their book *What is Parenthood*, Linda McClain and Daniel Cere use two contrasting models of parenthood: the integrative model and the diversity model. The *integrative model of parenthood* reflects a traditional, and still common, understanding of parenthood as a natural relation flowing from biological reproduction by one man and one woman within marriage (or legal adoption within marriage). It regards marriage between one man and one woman as the central social institution for integrating sexuality, reproduction, and parenthood so that children grow up with their two biological parents. The *diversity model* recognizes and responds to the growing diversity in patterns of family life. It acknowledges various pathways to parenthood. It defines parenthood more by the attachment bond between adult and child than by whether a marital relationship exists between two opposite-sex adults or there is a genetic tie between adult and child.

Stephanie Coontz, professor of history and family studies at Evergreen State College, points out that married people are generally happier, healthier and better protected against economic setbacks and emotional problems than people in other living arrangements. She suggests that some of these benefits might appear because people who already are socially skilled, economically self-sufficient, healthy and emotionally stable are more likely to marry and stay married than those with fewer of these qualities.

Marriage as a Social Institution

Different family styles have always existed in the Western world but the traditional sequence has been marriage, mortgage and children. Families are expected to nurture children rather than exploit them as laborers. Traditional marriage is a way to legitimize parenthood and to support foresight and self-sufficiency. It organizes fathers and mothers around nurturing the development of children.

Now decisions about marriage and parenting are made by the individuals rather than extended families or traditions. People marry spouses who they think will please them. If that doesn't happen, they assume they chose the wrong partner and divorce. Under no-fault policies, courts no longer need to justify a divorce.

Marriage has become a wager people are drawn into through sexual attraction and personal friendship. If things don't work out, the bet is lost and each party is free to end the relationship. The theme is that there is no reason to prefer one lifestyle over another for childrearing. Nobel Laureate Toni Morrison in a *Time* magazine interview expressed this clearly.

> The little nuclear family is a paradigm that just doesn't work.
> It doesn't work for white or black people. Why we are hanging
> on to it, I don't know.

Paula Ettelbrick, Executive Director of the International Gay and Lesbian Human Rights Commission, put it this way:

> Marriage of all institutions is to the liberationists a form of
> imprisonment; it reeks of a discourse that has bought and sold
> property, that has denigrated and subjected women, that has
> constructed human relationships into a crude and suffocating
> form.

In 2002, the Supreme Judicial Court of Massachusetts rejected the idea that marriage is centrally connected with bearing and raising children.

> The Commonwealth affirmatively facilitates bringing children
> into a family regardless of whether the intended parent is mar-
> ried or unmarried, whether the child is adopted or born into a
> family, whether assisted technology was used to conceive the
> child, and whether the parent or her partner is heterosexual,
> homosexual, or bisexual.

This view clearly removes marriage as the preferred venue for procreation.

Still for college-educated Americans, the motive to marry appears to have grown stronger in recent years. For others, marriage continues to be unappealing. David Popenoe, founder of the National Marriage Project, believes that the "marriage gap" is generating greater social inequality. America is becoming a nation divided not only by unequal education and income levels but by unequal family structures. Kay Hymowitz, Manhattan Institute fellow, posits that the separation of marriage from childrearing threatens to turn our opportunity-rich republic into a hereditary caste society with a married prosperous class and an unmarried poor class.

The current debate about marriage boils down to whether or not it is the optimal context for childrearing. The empirical evidence cited in this chapter says that it is. Despite the advantages of a child-free life, the desire for children and adult companionship remains strong in the majority of human beings.

Statistics

In 2011 51% of all adults were married. Many who marry are not interested in parenthood. Fortunately, neither the survival of the species nor individual fulfillment depends upon every person becoming a parent. Fewer families today fit the traditional image of two married parents living with their genetic children. In 2011:

- Of all households, 33% included children;

- Of households including children 66% consisted of married couples; 26% consisted of mother only homes; and 7% consisted of father only homes.

- 21% of married couples and 59% of unmarried couples have children from more than one relationship.

Marica Carlson and Paula England point out in *Changing Families in an Unequal Society* that, except for college-educated Americans, marriage continues to be less appealing. Individuals are marrying later and cohabiting more often. This trend contributes to an increasing gap in wellbeing between college-graduate married families and less-educated unmarried families.

The U.S. Marriage Index measures the integrity of marriage as a social institution. Between 1970 and 2008, the index dropped from 76 to 60. Only 53% percent of couples who married between 1975 and 1979 reached their silver anniversary.

In 2011, 49% of all married mothers were employed full time and 18% part time. Sixty-six percent of single mothers were employed full time and 18% part time. In 2010, 41% of all births were to unmarried girls and women (20% one-parent and 21% cohabiting) with 59% of births occurring with married couples.

Attitudes

A 2007 Pew survey found that Americans of all ages believe the link between marriage and parenthood has weakened. Just 41% of Americans said children are "very important" to a successful marriage, down from 65% in 1990. Children have fallen to eighth out of nine things people associate with successful marriages, well behind "sharing household chores, good housing, adequate income, happy sexual relationship, and faithfulness."

On the other hand, the Michigan Study of Adolescent Life Transitions revealed that despite greater acceptance of divorce, premarital sex and non-marital cohabitation since the 1960s, positive attitudes toward marriage and parenthood remain strong among high school seniors. Eighty-eight percent of male and 83% of female seniors said it was quite or extremely important to have a good marriage and family life.

In 2003 75% of college freshmen named raising a family as an important life goal, up from 59% in 1977. However, only 1 in 1,000 chose full-time homemaker as their probable career. Almost 70% of adolescent boys and 54% of girls agreed it's better for a person to get married than to go through life being single. They also felt that divorce is not the best solution to marital problems.

A Child Trends survey found that adolescents knew that a healthy relationship should be marked by respect, honesty, fidelity, good communication and the absence of violence. At the same time, many expressed pessimism about their chances of ever experiencing that type of relationship. Nor did they know many adults whose romantic relationships were worthy of emulation.

In a National Marriage Project survey, men expressed a desire to marry but were in no hurry to do so because they:

- Can get sex without marriage more easily than in the past;
- Can have a companion by cohabiting rather than marrying;

- Want to avoid divorce and its financial risks;

- Are waiting for the perfect soul mate;

- Face few social pressures to marry;

- Are reluctant to marry a woman who already has children; and

- Want to own a house before marrying.

More than half of the young men surveyed reported changing jobs and a variety of living arrangements including returning to their parents' homes. Male friends were their stable attachments.

Adolescent Parenthood and Marriage

Despite a nearly one-third decline over the past decade in adolescent pregnancy and birth rates in the United States according to the National Campaign to Prevent Teen Pregnancy:

- 60% of all girls age fifteen through seventeen and 73% of ages eighteen to nineteen approve of unwed childbearing.

- Half of all first unwed births are to adolescents.

- Within one year of childbirth, 8% of adolescent mothers marry the genetic fathers.

- Only 30% of adolescent mothers who do marry are still in that marriage at the age of 40.

COHABITATION

Over the years, marriage has lost ground as the context for childrearing and become more exclusively an intimate relationship between adults. The transition has come through piecemeal changes with little consideration of the social consequences of a weaker connection between marriage and childrearing.

The ethos of individualism has made unmarried cohabitation the lifestyle of choice for many young people. Formerly referred to as "shacking up" or "living in sin," cohabitation has become common. In 2006-2008, 58% of women ages nineteen to forty-four had cohabited. Cohabitation apparently functions as a substitute for being single rather than as a substitute for marriage or parenthood.

In 1994, two-thirds of respondents under the age of thirty in the National Survey of Families and Households felt that unmarried sex, cohabitation and unmarried births were socially acceptable. In 2001, 88% of young men and 93% of young women agreed that it is usually a good idea for a couple to live together before getting married. More than 50% of boys and girls now believe that having a child out of wedlock is an acceptable lifestyle that doesn't affect anyone else.

A 2012 analysis of the Princeton Fragile Families and Child Wellbeing Study suggests there are only slight negative implications for children raised in stable two-genetic-parent cohabiting families compared to stable two-genetic-married-parent families. The difference appears to be largely due to differences in the backgrounds of parents who choose cohabitation over marriage. Once these personal factors are taken into account, children of both kinds of stable parental relationships appear similar in terms of behavior problems. Children of cohabiting genetic parents who marry after childbirth appear no better off than the children of cohabiting genetic parents who remain unmarried as long as the relationship of the latter is stable.

On the one hand, these findings might indicate that marital unions are no more beneficial to children than cohabiting unions of biological parents as long as the relationship remains stable. On the other hand, marriages are more stable than cohabiting relationships. In cohabiting families, children move in and out of different family arrangements more often. The empirical fact is that cohabitation preceding marriage does not ensure a stable marriage later on.

ONE-PARENT HOMES

Although it might not seem so at first, the words used to describe contemporary families are important. Two-parent homes occur with and without marriage. When one parent is a nonresident, a family can be located in two homes. When a mother and father live separately, single-parent family doesn't accurately define the situation since one-parent homes can serve a two-parent family because the other parent lives elsewhere. Each can be with or without genetic parents. No wonder the word *family* confuses children, parents and researchers.

When parenthood generally referred to married adults, single parenthood resulted from the death or divorce of a parent. Adolescent parenthood was not formally recognized. In recent decades, personal choice has replaced cultural traditions in defining parenthood. Married parents now feel less obliged to stay together for the sake of their children. Separation usually is stressful for children but so is relentless conflict that is not resolved by counseling.

Currently, most parents are not single by death or divorce. According to the National Center for Health Statistics, the number of babies born to unwed women in their thirties and forties rose by 290% from 1980 to 2002. At some point in their lives, half of all children born in the United States will have lived in one-parent homes, primarily headed by women. More than half of those will live in poverty for a time and will continue the cycle of family disadvantage.

The organization Single Mothers by Choice is a support network for single women who have children without a relationship with a man. Three-quarters conceived with donor sperm. Their members typically are career women in their thirties or forties who decided to give birth or adopt knowing they would be their child's sole parent. Biological pressure meant they could no longer wait for marriage before starting a family. They became pregnant accidentally or from donor insemination, or they adopted a child. They seek men as out-of-home "social capital" (father figures) for their children.

Whether parents in the United States are married, cohabiting or raising children without a partner, they are more likely to change living arrangements than parents in the rest of the Western world. Compared to Canada, sixteen times as many children in the U.S. have had three or more men living with their mothers by the age of fifteen.

Over the past forty years, the greater financial independence of women contributed to the increase in one-parent homes facilitated by: 1) the decline in family size; 2) the increase in divorce rates; 3) expansion of the service sector where most women are employed; 4) an increase in women's earnings; and 5) civil rights legislation. These trends improved women's occupations as well as their earnings.

National social policies influence the wellbeing of children in one-parent homes. Countries with low single-mother poverty rates have a combination of child allowances, guaranteed child support, unemployment assistance, and housing allowances for low-income families that benefit both one- and two-parent homes.

Without an impossible experiment where children are randomly assigned to different kinds of families, we don't know how children in one-parent homes would have fared if they had lived with two genetic parents. Most one-parent homes raise their children successfully; however, their children do have more problems than those raised in two-parent homes.

The reason a home has only one parent is important. Kevin Lang, professor of economics at Boston University, and Jay Zagorsky, professor of economics at Ohio State University, found little evidence that the death of a parent affects children's economic wellbeing in adulthood. However, a mother's death might reduce a girl's cognitive performance while a father's death might lower a son's chances of marriage.

Although children of divorced parents have more adjustment problems than children of parents who never divorced, the divorce itself might not be the cause. Many of the problems seen in children of divorce can be accounted for by experiences in earlier years such as marital conflict, violence and inadequate parenting.

Impact on Children

The Princeton Fragile Families Project has established the fact that one-parent homes are associated with a host of problems. This is especially true if the parents are uneducated and unemployed. Poverty forces mothers to rear children in neighborhoods with high rates of unemployment, school dropouts, adolescent pregnancy and crime.

Children who live in one-parent homes have lower academic achievement than those in two-parent homes. Controlling for age, gender and grade level, secondary school students living in one-parent homes score lower on mathematics and science tests than those in two-married-parent homes. Children in stepparent homes score somewhat higher than one-parent homes but children living with two genetic parents score the highest. Those who live with their mother and an unmarried, non-genetic, cohabitating partner score the lowest.

Children living with both genetic parents remain in school longer than children in one-parent homes. High school graduation rates were 90% for those in two genetic-parent homes, 75% for those in divorced-mother homes and 69% for those in unwed-mother homes.

Children with absent fathers are more likely to drop out of school than children who live with their fathers. 71% of children who lived with two genetic parents go to college compared to 50% of children living only with their mothers. Each additional year spent with a single mother reduces a child's educational attainment by half a year, as does time spent in stepparent families.

Some of the impacts are much riskier. Children who spend part of their childhood in a single-mother home are twice as likely to have sex at an early age as children who live with both genetic parents. Daughters from single-mother homes also begin marital and non-marital childbearing at a younger age.

Whereas girls from two-parent homes have a 6% chance of having a child outside marriage by the age of twenty, chances for girls from divorced single-mother and unwed families are 11% and 14% respectively. Girls in stepfamilies have a 16% chance of unwed childbirth.

Growing up in a single-mother home is strongly linked to income later in life. Timothy Biblarz and Adrian Raftery found in *Family Structure, Educational Attainment, and Socioeconomic Success* that children from high occupational status homes were less likely to end up in high status occupations if they came from a single-mother home. Sara McLanahan and Gary Sandefur reported in *Growing Up with a Single Parent* that adults from single-mother homes were more likely to be unemployed and on welfare than those from two-parent homes.

A Father's Absence

A meta-analysis of the literature on father absence by the Princeton Center for Research on Child Wellbeing found lower levels of behavioral problems in adolescents living with married genetic parents than with all other family styles.

While over 90% of all American children live with their genetic mothers at some time, only about 50% spend at least part of their lives with their genetic fathers. Children who do not live with their genetic fathers often are disadvantaged by low income and poor relationships between and with their parents.

The annual expenditures made by the federal government to support father-absent homes total $100 billion a year. These expenditures include thirteen means tested benefit programs and child support enforcement.

Growing up without two parents who support each other is a significant contributor to drug abuse and delinquency. This is especially true when accompanied by poverty. When fathers are absent, children might be less well monitored because their mothers work longer hours.

Children who live apart from their genetic fathers are more likely to use illegal substances and to be arrested. Children below the age of fifteen who live in a household without a father are 70% more likely to commit crimes and 28% more likely to use marijuana than children who live with both genetic parents. Children living apart from their genetic fathers are 19% more likely to smoke cigarettes than others.

Children with behavior problems might push fathers away while well-behaved children might draw them in. But the behavior of parents has a greater effect on children than the behavior of children has on parents. Even if fathers become more involved, their children's behavioral problems might not decrease.

When nonresident fathers maintain a high-quality relationship with their children, some of the negative consequences of their absence can be attenuated. Currently there is interest in using social policies to strengthen father-family involvement, such as through counseling, mentoring, marriage education, enhancing relationship and parenting skills and fostering economic stability.

Impact on Girls

When fathers are absent, girls have few opportunities to learn how to relate to males. A father-daughter relationship sets the stage for her romantic choices, shapes her sexuality and influences her sense of herself as a woman. Developing an affectionate attachment with her father is important as a girl works through the Electra complex in which she fantasies marrying her father and displacing her mother. By working through this process, she comes to terms with the fantasy's impracticality.

Without a father's dependable involvement in her life, a girl lacks a model of adult male-female relationships as well as a tangible model of healthy masculinity. Daughters need father figures who can be counted on away from or at home. When they do not receive the attention and affection they desire from a father, they might seek it elsewhere. This quest leads to early and unstable relationships. The situation is compounded when mothers are depressed. The following was written by thirteen-year-old Crystal for the National Center for Fathering:

> I see my father a lot in my dreams but never does he turn around. I call for him, but he's just walking away. Every time I blow out the candles on my birthday cake, I wish that stranger would turn around and look at me. Maybe if he saw all the pain and suffering from living without him in my eyes, he would become a part of my life.

At the same time, if the relationship between father and daughter is too intense, a father might become the admired male in her life. She fulfills the Electra fantasy by becoming his primary love. When an incestuous relationship actually occurs, a girl suffers the consequences of sexual abuse. Her later life as a wife and a mother is adversely affected.

Children raised without a biological father have earlier average ages of first sexual intercourse than children raised in households where the father is present.

Both girls and boys might feel their fathers left their home because they didn't love them. One son put it this way: "A dad wouldn't leave a good kid, so it must have been my fault."

Impact on Boys

Boys usually first identify with their mothers. When a father is not available, boys have difficulty resolving the Oedipal complex in which they fantasize marrying their mothers and displacing the fathers. They cannot readily shift their identification from mother to father. This can lead to guilt over their unresolved fantasies. Repression of their masculinity might result. They can have difficulty developing and sustaining self-respect, forming lasting emotional attachments, recognizing their feelings and expressing themselves later with adult partners and their own children.

Boys also might focus on their fathers' faults as a way to deny their need for a father. One boy said he could prove he didn't need his father. Before taking any action, he imagined what his father would do and did the opposite. He claimed, "I don't need anyone." In contrast, another boy on the verge of tears described his feelings about his absent father:

> If my dad was still around, I wouldn't do so much dumb stuff. I'm pretty sure I'd be a good student. I'd have friends that were better for me. When I turn into a dad, I'm going to be different from my dad.

On the other hand, boys can contradict the stereotype that a boy suffers without a man in the home by growing into successful men. Journalist Peggy Drexler interviewed a group of what she called "maverick moms," relatively affluent and highly educated lesbians and single mothers by choice who were raising sons in San Francisco. The boys were socially savvy and generous while also being passionate about sports and roughhousing. Still, the families she interviewed were on society's fringes. Drexler viewed those maverick moms as pioneers of a new parenting style. They reject social judgments about family structure and gender stereotypes, and stress communication, community and love.

Perspectives on fathers

In their own minds, no boy or girl is without a dad. In the absence of fathers, they make up their own images. Even when disappointed or abused by their fathers, children may create images of loving fathers in order to bolster their own self-respect. Eleanor Roosevelt wrote about her love for her father in spite of his alcoholism and abandonment of her.

When fathers are rarely or never seen, children depend on their mothers or other relatives for information about them. If a mother speaks about an absent father realistically, a child is more likely to develop a positive image in spite of the father's failings. She might despise him but, if his problems can be understood, a child can develop a realistic image. This also applies to absent mothers.

Absent fathers miss an important developmental experience. Engaged fatherhood promotes a man's ability to understand himself, to understand others and to integrate his feelings in intimate relationships with family members. Fathers are more likely to give back to their communities than childless men.

Most absent fathers pay support and are in touch with their children. Some might feel that mothers claim support for themselves rather than the children. If mothers fail to accept or sustain father-child relationships, the fathers can feel frustrated and victimized.

When fathers see themselves as victims whose rights are ignored, they become resistant and disengaged. Non-payment of child support can be seen as a father's defiance or a moral failing. In a study of divorced, non-custodial "deadbeat fathers," they agreed that "bad" fathers existed but that applied to others not themselves. They accepted an obligation to contribute to their children's support but often deemed the amount or its terms unfair.

WHITHER PARENTHOOD?

In recent decades, parenthood has been increasingly defined by choice. Single parenthood, cohabitation, divorce, gay-lesbian relationships and re-marriage have created a variety of family life styles. Strong currents operate against both our cultural values and the scientific knowledge that affirm children's need for the love and nurturing of both parents. As the significance of marriage has declined, single parenthood by choice or necessity has become common.

Marriage has supported middle-class foresight, planning and self-sufficiency. It has organized men and women around nurturing children's cognitive, emotional and physical development. Now it separates successful middle-class children with both parents from their less-parented, under-achieving lower-class peers. The United States appears to be moving toward a *de facto* hereditary caste society based on family structure.

We need to make major adjustments in our social contract with them to give parents a greater return for their investment in children. Because stable families produce productive citizens, our social contract should strengthen families. Because raising children is a public good, our social contract should support parenthood.

Children prick our consciences. They painfully remind us that we are their flawed models, yet they also evoke our highest ideals. Although conflicts between the interests of older and younger generations are inevitable, the American cultural tradition is to promote competent parenthood. Still, there is a hidden barrier to achieving this goal—juvenile ageism.

Chapter Five

Juvenile Ageism

*Youth is a wonderful thing. What a crime to waste it
on children!*

GEORGE BERNARD SHAW

George Bernard Shaw opened the door to understanding where young people really stand in our society. Even children might smile at Shaw's cynical humor. However, if the word *Jews*, *blacks* or *gays* is substituted for *children*, prejudice is instantly apparent. The fact that we don't take offense at this slur against children illustrates how ingrained our prejudice is against them.

When I point this out, you still will likely doubt the existence of juvenile ageism. After all, we're just referring to children, and they aren't protesting...or so it seems. More to the point, why should anyone suggest prejudice and discrimination when children receive so much media attention and often are overindulged at home? They are better off now than a century ago because we protect them with child labor and abuse and neglect laws. We spend billions on public education and on supporting teen parents.

But a different picture emerges if we heed the National Commission on Children. It concluded over twenty years ago that our nation was failing its children. The fact that we're still failing them is reflected in the violence, habitual crime and welfare dependency that plague our society today and the evidence presented in Chapter Two. *Our children are protesting the consequences of juvenile ageism indeed.*

Many people are weary of the claims of victims of racism, sexism, classism and elder ageism. They understandably feel that we do not need another -ism. They correctly believe that prejudice and discrimination always have been and always will be a part of the human condition. But public consciousness of racism, sexism and elder ageism has led to counteracting destructive -isms.

We need to think objectively about ageism as a destructive force. The history of racism, sexism and elder ageism might help answer why awareness of juvenile ageism is essential for our society's wellbeing.

HISTORIC PREJUDICES

There was a time when the exploitation of African-Americans in the United States was justified by the belief that they were naturally inferior, destined to servitude and ignorance. They were regarded as either a different kind of being or at an earlier stage of evolution than Caucasians. They had inferior emotional control and moral capacities like children. Education was wasted on them because they were incapable of learning. A male adult was called "boy" with all that word's implications. He was regarded as a child who needed guidance and direction.

Institutional racism in the South continued after the Civil War. It shifted from benevolent to malevolent form as blacks were lynched, and whites avoided prosecution for crimes against them. Their inferior education, medical care, jobs, housing, representation and legal services are documented in an extensive literature.

Largely due to The Civil Rights Movement of the 1950s and 1960s, blacks developed a positive group identity, and overt discrimination has been outlawed. Although racism remains a vital issue, substantial progress has been made to overcome it.

Women have been presumed to be weak, emotional, lacking ambition, illogical and unfit for managerial or technical jobs. They have been considered as dependent as children. Stereotypes denied women the educational and career opportunities available to men. To this day, the results are less pay for the same work and a glass ceiling that can limit workplace promotions.

Waves of feminist movements over the years culminated in equal rights legislation. Marriage is now characterized as a relationship between two individuals with equal personal rights. But just as blacks have shown prejudice against other blacks, women have shown prejudice against other women. This is most visible when discussing the priority given to homemaking and childrearing versus paid careers.

The public's awareness of sexism has extended beyond a single gender as prejudice and discrimination against males has begun to gain recognition, such as with boys in some female dominated classrooms.

Classism is prejudice and discrimination based on different social or economic groups. The family into which a person is born determines that person's place in society. The traditional example is India's caste system. Still an American birth family shapes every person's life almost as surely.

The Horatio Alger theme claims that anyone can achieve anything in America, so the existence of classism is usually denied. The predominant view of the United States is that of a classless meritocracy and a land of unbounded opportunity. The theme that anyone can become president was reinforced by the election of Barack Obama who wrote *Dreams from My Father: A Story of Race and Inheritance* as described in the following review:

> A brilliant but troubled Kenyan father abandoned his teenage bride and their infant son. Obama described a footloose mother who took "Barry" to Indonesia with a second husband, then shipped him back to Hawaii to live with his grandparents. He felt a sense of alienation as a young black man growing up with few African-American friends or role models. Chubby as a kid, wayward as a teen, he developed formidable personal discipline, down to his daily exercise routine and abstemious eating and drinking habits. He made a home for himself in Chicago and sought out the stability of marriage and fatherhood. He successfully pursued a career in politics.

Nevertheless, social class strongly influences destiny. Chuck Collins and Felice Yeskel demonstrate this in *Economic Apartheid in America: A Primer on Economic Inequality & Insecurity*. Contrary to popular belief, our nation was not established as a true democracy. Only white men who owned property initially had the right to vote.

Wealthy people have always enjoyed advantages over working class people. A popular myth is that the wealthy earn their fortunes through hard work and effort. Average Americans work very hard indeed, yet when adjusted for inflation, their wages have been in serious decline for years even as their productivity has increased. Workers are producing more and earning less. Meanwhile, corporate profits and CEO salaries based on corporate revenues have increased.

Classism occurs in both downward and upward directions. This is especially evident during political campaigns that exaggerate populism and elitism. Poor mothers are portrayed as "welfare queens", university professors are "out of touch with reality" and the wealthy are "conscienceless, money-grubbing pirates" who exploit the middle class.

AGEISM

In 1969, the physician Robert Butler described ageism as prejudice and institutional discrimination against the elderly in housing, employment and health care. More specifically, gerontophobia—fear of aging—was identified as a prejudice that led to discrimination by avoiding the elderly and elder abuse. In 1970, the Gray Panthers was created as an advocacy group to combat ageism. The following year, President Nixon condemned ageism in his address to the White House Conference on Aging.

The Group for the Advancement of Psychiatry identified ageism as avoidance of elders by younger individuals. This particular form of discrimination was created by a society "that regards death as a personal affront and that values the action, vigor, and skills of youth over the contemplation, experience, and wisdom of old age."

The elderly are presumed to be inferior in physical strength, in mental abilities and in their awareness of the surrounding world. They are considered dependent on others, like children, due to the physical and mental decline that accompanies aging. Intriguingly, elder abuse and neglect have been readily identified as reflecting ageism whereas childhood abuse and neglect have not. Of course, older persons are politically organized to protect their interests and claim abuse while the young are unrepresented and unable to protect their own interests.

Since the young and the old are both dependent on society, they actually have much in common. They are both financially dependent because they do not earn income. This can place the duty and the burden for their support on their families and government. They compete against each other for government funds. Unless elders are motivated by a sense of responsibility for the young and the future, their political power easily overwhelms the interests of the young and planning for our society's economic future. The duty of all adults to provide for the next generation is easily neglected in our political systems.

Sacrificing for our children's present and future wellbeing has inherent moral attraction. Still no platitude is more frequently invoked and more frequently disregarded when it comes time for action than "Do it for our kids."

Children have seldom been included in descriptions of ageism; even when they are, the references have been limited to young adults. Ironically, the educational literature for children refers to ageism only as it affects the elderly. Psychologist Todd Nelson's book *Ageism* defines juvenile ageism as the prejudice and discrimination of the young against the elderly. *This exclusion of children whose status is defined by age from ageism is the ultimate expression of juvenile ageism.*

Juvenile ageism actually was identified early in the last century. Maria Montessori called attention to the "universal prejudices" against children, particularly in the attitude that adults always know what's best for them. She cited the false assumptions that children must be taught to learn, which overlooks their innate thirst for learning; that children's minds are empty, which overlooks their rich imaginations; and that young children do not work, which overlooks the growth-inducing nature of play.

Obvious signs of juvenile ageism can be seen today in public displays. The *ChildFree Network* is a support group for adults without children. *How to be a Happy Parent...in Spite of Your Children* is a book title that needs no further comment. A newspaper ad urged readers: *If you don't own a kid, borrow one and catch "Great Big Tour" in the Oscar Mayer Theatre.* In the play *The Gingerbread House,* the father says, "Honey, I think we should sell our kids. We can start our lives again."

Again, imagine your response if the word *Jews*, *blacks* or *gays* was substituted for *children*.

Juvenile ageism is concealed by rhetoric that idealizes children even as we ignore their interests in adult affairs and their stake in our future economy. Our nation's failure to plan for the future of our children isn't considered the same kind of failure as parents' failure to plan for their daughters' and sons' futures. Because the prejudice and discrimination of juvenile ageism isn't recognized, we need to know more about these powerful hidden forces that victimize our young citizens.

VICTIMIZATION OF YOUNG PERSONS

Prejudice occurs when judgments are made before facts are determined and weighed. It refers to any unreasonable attitude of superiority over others and often is triggered by competition for space, material things or time.

Discrimination occurs when prejudiced people are given superior access to resources. Individuals are treated differently based on their group membership or category rather than on merit. Discrimination takes both individual and social forms. The first type consists of overt acts that harm others. The second type is more subtle and difficult to spot. This kind of covert discrimination operates within established and often respected influences in our society.

Discrimination is reinforced by the compliance of victims as well as their rebellious reactions. When victims lash out, they are blamed for the frustrations and guilt of the prejudiced. A clear-cut example is found with delinquent kids. They are victims of our society's failure to ensure that they have competent parents and safe neighborhoods. Their rebellious behavior is punished without addressing its obvious causes and our unrecognized guilt for ignoring their longstanding plight.

Victims of prejudice are treated differently because they are different in appearance, interests and sophistication. Children's natural physical, mental and resource inferiority makes them dependent on others and vulnerable to prejudice and discrimination. Their dependence along with their natural inclination to challenge authority make them prime targets when they compete with adults for space, resources, emotional involvement and time or when they make adults anxious.

Dependents of any age threaten our independence. They require personal sacrifices that change the status quo. The birth of a child alters a parent's life even more dramatically than an elderly parent's incapacity. Although affection for and commitment to a dependent person makes those sacrifices possible, the inevitable result is personal loss, inconvenience and some degree of resentment. In this context, a dependent person can be seen as inferior and less deserving than an independent adult. Dependent persons also are a burden for anyone who pays taxes.

What's more, prejudice and discrimination can be expressed in benevolent and idealizing ways. For example, before racism was considered a social problem, many people believed slaves were content and needed direction. Before sexism was challenged, many people believed women were dependent and were satisfied with a subservient status. The idealization of motherhood continues to help men avoid childrearing tasks with their own children.

Benevolent prejudice underlies the pro-children rhetoric that allows adults to feel good. Thinking and speaking about our devotion to children helps to conceal discrimination against them. It enables a lack of action that might fulfill our responsibilities. Benevolent ageism also allows us to believe that the elderly are better off receiving special care away from their families and that children are better off in educational environments away from their families.

Many of us believe the material wishes of our children should be gratified or that our children should have better lives than we did. We don't recognize that overly protective and indulgent attitudes prevent our children from learning how to handle life's challenges and opportunities. Because children really are dependent, the guise of protecting and indulging them conceals juvenile ageism. The harmful effects are less evident because children's missed opportunities and challenges don't occur until far into the future.

Benevolent juvenile ageism can take other forms. When children are viewed as capable, rational and independent in order to justify less parental involvement, they again become victims. Over the past thirty years, children's capabilities have increasingly been seen as better developed by professionals than by parents. This creates jobs in childcare and early childhood education and frees parents for paid employment.

These independent children can then achieve the American ideal of individual freedom. They quickly shed signs of their vulnerability, neediness or bewilderment as they adopt the cool persona of the sophisticated children in commercialized images. A common example is the teenage gangs' hip-hop lifestyle, which nurtures nihilism, misogyny and bravado and conceals insecurity and immaturity. All of this undermines childhood and adolescence as long, legitimate life stages during which our young prepare for fulfilling and responsible lives through cultural lessons provided by competent parents.

As long ago as 1983, the writer Marie Winn in *Children Without Childhood* called attention to children who grow up without experiencing childhood. The pressure placed on children to act like adults and its commercial exploitation is vividly illustrated by this 2011 anecdote from *Newsweek*:

> Five-year-old Olivia Myers is an indefatigable clothes horse. "She's had a great eye from a very early age," says her mother, Alyse. Take the flirty ensemble the youthful New Yorker angled off to school in last week. In low-slung, torso-tight flowered bell bottoms with a frothy white "poet" blouse from her favorite boutique, "Little Leepers," Olivia sashayed with the poise of any nubile Lolita bound for a discotheque—except she's about a third the size. "She's five and three quarter years old going on 15," says her mother proudly.

Premature introduction to sexual activity is an acknowledged example of the loss of childhood. One in five adolescents say they have electronically sent or posted online nude or seminude images of themselves. About 40% have had nude/seminude images originally meant to be private shared with them. An online survey by TRU indicates that more than a third say that exchanging sexy words and pictures makes "hooking up" with others more likely.

At the same time, Garrison Keillor noted that childhood and adolescence have been stolen by adults. Immaturity has become the norm rather than the exception. Men refuse to grow up; husbands in their thirties enjoy playing the same videogames that obsess twelve-year-olds; young men and women won't commit to marriage or family; and fathers fight with umpires or coaches at little league games. Keillor put it this way in *The Book of Guys*:

> Years ago, manhood was an opportunity for achievement, and now it is a problem to overcome...boy-men fixate on adolescent longings for the intensity and variety of experience and escape from their parents and family...over time they have abandoned traditional markers of male maturity and embraced perpetual adolescence. Commercial culture reinforces both trends.

Keillor's point is affirmed by Diana West in *The Death of the Grown-Up: How America's Arrested Development Is Bringing Down Western Civilization*.

Underlying the tendency to denigrate childhood is the disparagement of anyone who is small, weak or needy. We prize size, strength and self-sufficiency. As a result, childhood and adolescence tend to be regarded as necessary evils en route to adulthood. They are to be passed through as quickly as possible rather than be experienced as legitimate phases of life to be lived fully.

Arguments Against the Existence of Juvenile Ageism

The argument can be made that whatever difficulties America's children have individually or collectively don't reflect prejudice or discrimination. Adversity is part of life. Children and adults can suffer because they are innocent bystanders, as happens in war. Children and adults can fall victim to misfortune, poverty, bad parenting, racism and sexism. Child neglect and abuse can spring from parental deficiencies, illnesses or disorders without prejudice or discrimination.

The existence of juvenile ageism also can be dismissed on the grounds that parents represent the interests of their children. They may do so imperfectly but mistakes do not constitute prejudice or discrimination. The power adults have over children comes from their legal and socioeconomic privileges, greater resources and nurturing.

What's more, the interests of adults without children are becoming increasingly dominant. The interests of children who presumably are significant only to their parents can be overridden by the will of the majority. A tangible byproduct of this trend was the disappearance of the family wage by the equalization of pay for adults with and without children.

A particular objection to juvenile ageism is that our democratic republic is based upon competing interests in our political system. Since children aren't represented, their plight isn't a reflection of prejudice or discrimination; it's simply the result of governments that only represent registered voters.

Another objection is that unsafe neighborhoods and violence result from poverty and racism; the fact that children are affected is incidental. That attitude might be valid in underdeveloped nations but is unjustifiable in a prosperous society. We cannot claim ignorance or lack of resources as excuses for leaving our children unprotected from poverty and violence. Since the cost is miniscule compared to wars, national security and crime, we can easily access the resources to ensure their safety and competent parenting… if we have the will to do so.

Arguments for the Existence of Juvenile Ageism

In the distant past, fathers held life-and-death power over their children. Sons and daughters were regarded as property parents could treat as they wished. Over time, restrictions were placed on the rights of parents as societies became increasingly involved in the lives of children. Children have been accorded an increasing number of legal and civil rights over the last century.

The term *adultism* first appeared in psychological literature in 1933. It defined a child possessing the "physique and spirit" of an adult and who tended toward delinquency. In his seminal 1978 article "Adultism" in *Adolescence*, Jack Flasher redefined adultism as the belief that children are inferior. Adultism showed in excessive nurturing, possessiveness or over-restrictiveness consciously or unconsciously designed to control a child.

Adultism was expanded by the Child Welfare League of America to include disempowering and disenfranchising youth by viewing them as objects instead of human beings. President Theodore Roosevelt recognized this injustice when he initiated a series of White House Conferences on Children and Youth held from 1909 to 1971.

Juvenile ageism is a more descriptive and understandable term than *adultism*, which can be construed to mean prejudice against adults and *childism*, which can imply childish behavior and omits adolescents. *Juvenile ageism* identifies age as the target and links the young with older people who also must contend with elder ageism.

Prejudice and discrimination against children weren't described as juvenile ageism until the 1970s by Chester Pierce, a psychiatrist, and myself. In 1980, the pediatrician Michael Rothenberg suggested a hidden national conspiracy against children. As proof, he pointed out the vast discrepancy between pro-children rhetoric and the actions and inactions of our governments.

How does *juvenile ageism* explain the variety of ways children are mistreated? When is maltreatment the result of juvenile ageism and when is it the result of ignorance, incompetence or just plain meanness? When those factors explain the maltreatment, does that automatically exclude juvenile ageism? Is a mentally ill parent who abuses a child a juvenile ageist? Is our society's inability to protect everyone from violence a sign of juvenile ageism when children become victims?

Answers to these questions can be found by comparing juvenile ageism with racism and sexism. Ask if all the abuse, neglect and segregation of minorities and women can be blamed on racism and sexism. The answer clearly is no. Members of these groups can bring maltreatment upon themselves. They can be mistreated for reasons other than their race or gender.

We can identify the trends and instances that reflect the discriminatory practices of racism, sexism and ageism by looking at the attitudes that motivate behavior. First, attitudes that reflect in-group superiority over an out-group, coupled with the power to dominate out-group members, signal an -ism. Second, -ism-based behavior exploits, maltreats or ignores people's needs because their personal characteristics differ from the dominant group. Those differences can be based on race, gender, class or age.

In contrast, the maltreatment of others based on competition, conflicts of opinion or desires, envy or jealousy and revenge need not reflect an -ism. This means that *juvenile ageism exists when adults use their superior power to mistreat children as inferior persons in order to further their own needs and desires.* By the same token, elders can be the victims of ageism when younger people use their superior power to mistreat them to satisfy their own needs and desires.

Still, the idea of unequal treatment, which is central in racism and sexism, seems more complicated in juvenile ageism. Unlike racial and gender groups, children usually are inferior in mental and physical abilities. Children progress from complete dependency through obtaining increasing privileges and responsibilities. During that process, they require gradually diminishing supervision. Therefore juvenile ageism cannot be invoked when children are treated differently due to their immaturity.

However, the comparison of elder and juvenile ageism with racism and sexism holds up when equality means *equality in rights and opportunities*. Ageists claim that the rights and opportunities of elders and children are *less important* than those of the majority of adults. Children therefore can be treated unequally and their right to developmental opportunities can go unfulfilled. Elders also can be treated unequally and opportunities to meet their rights and needs can be ignored or denied.

Specific psychological factors foster ageism. Adults are naturally ambivalent toward the elderly and the young because both restrict their independence. The elderly remind us that we will age and die. The young remind us of our childlike, dependent tendencies. These directly conflict with the priority we place on being carefree and independent. To ward off those anxieties, we might avoid the elderly and expect our children to be independent.

At a deeper level, those of us who are parents naturally hold some resentment toward our children because they require sacrifices. This resentment is accentuated by the competition between careers and childrearing demands. What's more, many of us harbor shards of the frightened, hurt or angry children we once were. This blocks true empathy with our children and creates either excessive anger or overprotection.

Most importantly, the premise held by adults without offspring that parents do not merit special consideration solely due to childrearing responsibilities denies the principle that all adults have a responsibility to support the continuation of our society through the next generation...*posterity* in the Declaration of Independence. It ignores the stake all adults have in preventing the costly products of struggling families: violence, habitual crime and welfare dependency.

JUVENILE AGEISM IN THE UNITED STATES

The prejudice and discrimination of both elder and juvenile ageism can be identified in how power is wielded over rights and opportunities in relationship to age. The triad of 1) exploitation that uses; 2) maltreatment that demeans; and 3) neglect that ignores dependency are forms of discrimination that reflect an attitude of superiority.

Exploitation That Uses

Juvenile ageism serves a variety of purposes. On the positive side, children can enhance a parent's self-esteem when they respect and need their parents. On the negative side, children can be exploited when having one is used to build self-esteem and when children are seen as sources of affection. Whenever they are used primarily to satisfy their parents' needs, children are exploited through their parents' superior power.

Parents exploit children when they project unacceptable parts of themselves onto their children. In this way, we avoid painful feelings about ourselves. This is frequently seen in the physical abuse of children perceived as threatening. Another form of exploitation is to take out resentments and hostility toward another adult, often the other parent, on a helpless child. Children can be expected to fulfill their parents' expectations rather than their own potential. Steven graphically illustrated this theme:

> Twenty-four-year-old Mary came to our clinic because eight-year-old Steven was unmanageable at home and at school. She was at her wits end and wanted "something done about Steven."

> Mary was raised in an abusive home as the oldest of five children. Because of her parents' alcoholism and unpredictability, she raised her younger siblings. In the eyes of her mother she could "never do anything right." Her father hit her during alcohol-induced rages. She managed to get by in school and parent her siblings when her mother was intoxicated. When she was sixteen, she deliberately became pregnant in order to get away from home. Her marriage ended in the first year because of her husband's irresponsibility and abuse. A series of relation-

ships with unstable males followed, each one ending because they exploited her.

In family therapy, Mary revealed with a flood of tears her frightening insight that she had been taking out her longstanding resentment against males who exploited her on Steven. She could see that she was prejudiced against Steven and had been discriminating against him. Steven was transfixed by his mother's emotions. He hadn't seen her cry this way before. He went to her and put his arms around her. They both cried together. With this reframing of the relationship between mother and son, Mary no longer needed to be a perpetrator. Steven no longer had to rebel as the victim of her prejudice and discrimination.

Mary and Steven are familiar to family therapists who commonly uncover scapegoating in families. The rebellion of the victim can be remedied by a more realistic and accepting attitude from the perpetrator. Understanding that you're prejudiced is the first step toward overcoming discrimination.

Many abusive parents were abused as children. When they abuse their sons and daughters, they are reacting to distorted views. They often expect their children to be "ideal parents" who give them love and respect. They feel betrayed when their children are just children who need guidance and make demands upon them.

Do distorted expectations mean that behavior is not prejudiced and discriminatory? Is a mentally ill parent who abuses a child a juvenile ageist? These questions can be answered by examining racism and sexism. Certainly many personal determinants exist in those -isms. Adults who have been discriminated against can be prejudiced themselves. In racism, darker-skinned blacks can be prejudiced against people with lighter skin and vice versa. Insecure men dominate women. The essential question is whether abusive parents deny their children's rights and opportunities to serve their own needs. If the answer is yes, they are juvenile ageists.

Teachers, clergypersons, coaches, physicians, psychotherapists and other adults in authority can abuse their power, especially when a child or adolescent offers affection or respect that is perceived as seductive. Under those

circumstances, exploitative juvenile ageism occurs when the adult with superior power has an exploitative sexual relationship with a young person.

Maltreatment that Demeans

The most glaring forms of discrimination in juvenile ageism are vi-
olations of civil rights that would be regarded as rejection, segregation,
harassment, oppression, violence, torture and murder if they targeted an
adult. Lumping together all these egregious offences under child abuse and
neglect—a less evocative term—demeans children. Significantly, the death
of a child from abuse often is not regarded as murder, and the word torture
never is used to describe child abuse, even when children are chained in
basements and beaten.

Most explanations for child neglect and abuse focus on socioeconomic
and racial factors as if the quality of parenting played a minor role. Parental
pathology, although recognized, is explained away as a reaction to stressful
or disadvantaged circumstances. We especially demean children by solely
blaming them rather than their parents when they become social problems
and deal with them as if they were adult offenders.

Prejudice against children also is more subtly reflected in the demeaning attitude that children don't deserve more than their parents can provide.
Inherent in this view is the belief that children are personal possessions of
their parents without their own interests or rights. Children from disadvantaged families therefore don't deserve the same rights and opportunities as
children from affluent families. "They don't deserve my support as a taxpayer.
They aren't like me."

One of the reasons we do not act to prevent child neglect and abuse is
that we are reluctant to judge parental competence. This gives parents an
unchallenged superior position and enables them to exercise power over
their children through neglect and abuse. By failing to prevent the familial
and environmental factors associated with neglect and abuse we are with-
holding the power to protect (neglecting) children. It is an expression of
juvenile ageism. Punishing children who are reacting to parental neglect
and abuse is an even more clear-cut expression of juvenile ageism.

Neglect that Ignores Dependency

Is juvenile ageism really expressed when our society fails to protect our children from parental neglect and abuse? Here again the answer lies in the attitude. Do we regard our children as human beings with rights or as the personal property of their parents? Does ignoring incompetent parents reflect a dehumanizing attitude accompanying our adult superiority when we fail to exercise our power to protect our children before they are damaged by neglect and or abuse?

Protests against animal abuse are easily organized but have you ever heard of an organized protest against child abuse? We could explain that absence because animals are helpless and need protection. We could claim we don't know what to do about child abuse. We could say that childrearing is a totally private matter with no consequences for society. We could say that child neglect and abuse aren't related to society's violence, habitual crime or welfare dependency. But we know that none of these statements are true.

Incompetent parents obviously neglect and abuse children. Yet we don't recognize incompetent parenting as a public health and national economic risk even though it's more important than environmental toxins, poverty, malnutrition and missed immunizations. If we seriously want to prevent child neglect and abuse, we need to acknowledge 1) that we do know about the problem; 2) that we do know what to do about it; and 3) that we have the power to act preventively. By failing to act until children and adolescents are damaged, we are dehumanizing children from a position of adult superiority that could be—but is not—used to protect them.

Another kind of exploitation that ignores children's developmental needs and opportunities is giving a higher priority to the paid work of mothers than to the unpaid work of nurturing their babies. State welfare-to-work policies can require a mother to return to work after her baby is six-weeks-old even though childcare at that age costs more than parental care and the income generated by employment, making maternal care and breastfeeding less expensive than childcare. This policy underlines the belief that paid work is more important to society than unpaid parenting even when its costs taxpayers more.

In *What Money Can't Buy: Family Income and Children's Life Chances* Susan Mayer points out that the first rule of policy-making should be *don't*

promulgate a policy that will interfere with social bonding. A higher priority
is given in public policies to parental income and childcare than to attachment bonding. Paid work is more highly valued even when a policy
incurs higher immediate and long-term costs for taxpayers. Because such
a policy costs more, it isn't based on economics. Instead, it reflects a prejudice against mothers who are receiving welfare and want to meet the developmental needs of their babies, as if mothering is not essential for their
babies. This prejudice extends to employed mothers and fathers who do not
have paid parental leaves as well.

Children as Commodities

In another vein, artificial insemination and childbearing are colored by the
assumption that children are commodities. Embryos and fetuses are referred to as the "products of conception." Many workers, including labora-
tory technicians, physicians, lawyers and surrogate mothers, labor in this
industry that produces and markets these human commodities.

The production of a baby through *in vitro* fertilization can involve five
separate persons: the female genitor, the male genitor, the female surrogate, the functional mother and the functional father. Each person brings
new rights and duties to an enterprise in which the interests of the potential children are seldom considered. Accordingly, the state of Victoria in
Australia was the first common-law jurisdiction to regulate infertility technologies. The Supreme Court of France outlawed surrogate motherhood
entirely, holding that it violates a woman's body and undermines adoption.

In the United States, surrogacy is largely unregulated. In *Building a
Baby with Few Ground Rules*, Stephanie Saul calls attention to the emerging commercial market for surrogate babies. Vexing ethical questions are
raised. As a result, the American Bar Association has developed a model
act for state legislatures. One section of the proposal holds that when prospective surrogate mothers have no genetic link to the babies, court pre-
approval, including a home study, would be required.

Meanwhile, being admitted to California's Cryobank as a sperm donor
is like getting into Harvard. The bank accepts fewer than one percent of its
26,000 applicants every year. One donor Googled his donor number. After
locating a baby generated from his sperm, he sold a photo of the child to

Cryobank for $200 so they could show how his offspring would look. The mother of that baby had already located two other babies. An impromptu on-line community of mothers who had used his sperm formed. As his sperm sold out quickly he received $10,000.

A recent documentary on the Style network featured a donor who knows of at least 70 offspring from his donations. The implications for the scores of biologically related children and donors who can easily find each other have not been considered. In an Institute for American Values study *My Daddy's Name Is Donor: A New Study of Young Adults Conceived Through Sperm Donation*, forty-five percent felt bothered by the circumstances of their conception and that money was exchanged in order to conceive them.

In *The Revolution in Parenthood: The Emerging Global Clash between Adult Rights and Children's Needs*, Elizabeth Marquardt points out that when society changes marriage, it also changes parenthood. The divorce revolution and the rise in single-parent childbearing weakens father-child ties and introduces a host of rotating players called parents. The assisted reproductive technologies first used by married heterosexual couples and later by singles and same-sex couples raise still more uncertainties. The true meaning of motherhood and fatherhood comes into question, and children are exposed to new stressors and losses the adults never foresaw. The interests and rights of children are ignored...even possibly deliberately dismissed.

Where Are We Going?

Juvenile ageism permits us to have laws and social policies in which the genetic mother-father model is being replaced with the idea that babies, children and adolescents can do well with any caregivers...after all they can and must adapt to our adult world. This idea flies in the face of the developmental needs and rights of children described later in Chapter Eight but first brings us to juvenile ageism in our society.

Chapter Six

Juvenile Ageism in Society

My own personal view, as a magistrate, is that our society intervenes far too late in the process of antisocial behavior as this develops in children. It is much easier, and more viable, to make rules in the homes and at school and enforce these, than to try rehabilitation programs on adults whose lives have been ruined by society's unwillingness to get involved until it is too late for the life habit of crime to be reversed.

MAGISTRATE SYBIL B. G.
EYSENCK, 1989

The categories of societal juvenile ageism are:

1) When children are ignored as citizens with developmental needs as important as the needs and desires of adults.
2) When children are unnecessarily segregated from public places and public media;
3) When adolescents are treated as adults.
4) When services for children do not serve the interests of children.

5) When child development research is biased against the developmental needs of children.

6) When public programs place parental wishes above children's interests.

AGEISM THAT IGNORES CHILDREN AS CITIZENS

The fact that debates occur over whether or not children are full-fledged citizens is a reflection of juvenile ageism. Children don't vote, and families with children are a minority in our society. It's therefore difficult for our political system to address their fundamental needs and problems. Our political system inherently tends to discriminate against children because they are not effectively represented. Parents do not have an extra vote for each child. Our political system discriminates against our children when its superior power advances adult interests while ignoring our responsibility to protect and further the interests of our children...the next generation.

Prejudice and discrimination are fostered by the dominance of self-centered individualism and consumerism in our society. Encouraging financial success without concern for the wellbeing of others breeds self-indulgence and exploitation. The short-term satisfaction of personal desires takes an increasing priority over long-term commitments to spouses and parenthood. The young are seen as burdens or exploitable consumers rather than as the next generation.

A prime example of the impact of individualism on families comes from childless taxpayers. They argue that child tax deductions unfairly shift the tax burden to them. One taxpayer without children complained, "I have been working since I was fifteen to support myself and am sick of families receiving aid." Another taxpayer said, "Those with more children use more services and should be taxed more heavily, rather than given a tax break."

Whenever the interests of adults and children conflict, adult interests almost always prevail, as if children are not citizens of equal standing. Unlike other minority or oppressed groups, children cannot claim their rights. In 1977 the Carnegie Council on Children in *All Our Children: The American Family under Pressure* presciently declared:

...until policy makers and planners shift their focus to the broad ecological pressures on children and their parents, our public policies will be unable to do much more than help individuals repair the damage that environment is constantly re-inflicting on them.

Then as today virtually the last question we ask of any public policy is how it will affect our children. It should be the first question. Eugene Steuerle, an economist with the Urban Institute, points out that our nation's budget reflects priorities in which children, investment and, more generally, our posterity rank low. The interests of children are inevitably neglected in budgetary crossfires.

The Partnership for America's Economic Success report *Investing in Children* projects that domestic spending on education and research will fall from 7.9% in 2007 to 6.2% in 2017. The children's portion will drop from 2.3% to 1.8%. The Brookings Institution and Urban Institute's *Report on Federal Expenditures on Children Through 2010* projected that the children's share of the federal budget would drop from 11% to 8% in 2020 as mandated spending rises, especially for Social Security and Medicare.

These trends will aggravate the current plight of our children and youth that was predicted in the 1989 Report of the U.S. Select Committee on Children, Youth and Families. Two years later, the National Commission on Children pointed out "that the most prosperous nation in the world seems to be failing its children." The generally low priority set by federal, state and county funding for vulnerable children, especially those who have been damaged by neglect and abuse, is a glaring example of societal juvenile ageism.

The associate director of the Milwaukee Department of Human Services pointed out that it's easier to get money for a penguin exhibit at the zoo than for child protection. For each $10.00 of Milwaukee County property taxes, the park system receives $2.01, the museum $0.36, the zoo $0.15, the performing arts center $0.12, the symphony $0.07 and child protection services $0.04. There are "friends" of museums and "friends" of zoos at budget appropriation hearings but there are no "friends" of abused and neglected children.

Another example of ignoring the direct impact adult affairs have on children occurs when their interests aren't considered sufficiently during divorce proceedings. Many children become victims of inadequate and unpaid child support. The moral and legal obligation of parents to financially support their children is ignored when those obligations are treated the same as unpaid credit card debts. The lack of enforcement amounts to societal support of child neglect. This has been recognized by the recent federal requirement that states vigorously enforce child support obligations.

AGEISM THAT SEGREGATES CHILDREN

The most pervasive form of societal juvenile ageism is the exclusion of children from public aspects of our society. Obviously, children and adults live in different worlds. Children's worlds are defined by their parents and the limited range of their environments. Children therefore can be denied access to a private adult world. Parents can restrict access to their bedrooms. Society also can designate certain places as adult-only. It does not follow that children should be denied access to public places or media that should be accessible to all citizens regardless of race, creed, gender or age.

In order to protect children from unsafe public places and from the undesirable influences of movies, television programs and magazines, certain public aspects of society are off limits to children. The emphasis is on excluding children from harmful influences rather than on creating a society in which children can freely participate. When we define our tolerance of public behavior, we act as though children are not members of the public. We set limits of tolerance according to the lowest adult standards rather than standards appropriate for children. We act as if children do not exist.

This exclusion means that children are denied free access to public places, public information and public entertainment so that adults can have free access to activities that are harmful to children. The constitutional right to free expression by adults often is pitted successfully against the need to protect children from pornography and violent images, as if children did not have rights. Instead of designating private places and media for adults, we segregate one-quarter of the population from public places and media. In effect, we create an unnecessarily segregated world for children.

Rather than creating a society with a suitable public atmosphere for our young citizens, parents are expected to protect and segregate their children from unsuitable public influences. In 2009, the U.S. Supreme Court refused to hear an appeal of the 2000 Third Circuit Court of Appeals Decision in ACLU v. Reno II. The case blocked enforcement of the Child Online Protection Act, which established criminal penalties for online commercial distribution of material harmful to minors. The Appeals Court held that the Act was unconstitutional because it made every web communication provider abide by the most restrictive community's standards. Our societal, community and media standards would be quite different if all adults, including the justices of the U.S. Supreme Court, seriously considered how they are modeling values and behavior for our young citizens. Children and youth are watching all of us.

The rational that children should be segregated from unsafe places and undesirable public media rather than having society accommodate them was used to segregate women from the freewheeling "man's world." Fortunately, segregation and harassment of women in the armed forces and the workplace is no longer publicly tolerated. Both are expected to respectfully accommodate women. The same could be accomplished for children.

The segregation of children and youth can be compared to the same form of discrimination against adults. How would you respond to restricting the access of black adults, women, homosexuals or the physically handicapped to publicly sanctioned information, entertainment and events that were offensive or harmful to them? Few people would tolerate this, yet we tolerate, condone and promote events and materials that are offensive and harmful to one-quarter of our population...children and youth.

The only reasonable conclusion is that children are being treated as inferior beings rather than as citizens with age-appropriate rights comparable to those of adults. The most obvious consequence is the struggle of parents against violent and sexually stimulating societal influences. They are expected to protect their children from those public influences. They also are expected to gird their children against the dangers of public places and neighborhoods.

The most important example of self-destructive, societal juvenile ageism is indifference to the deteriorating quality of life of disadvantaged children and adolescents followed by punishing them for their behavior generated by incompetent parents and our society's failure to provide safe neighborhoods and schools. Our society has abandoned its role in protecting its young citizens. Except in rural and suburban areas, most children have lost the freedom of movement and association provided by safe neighborhoods.

In a survey conducted for *Children Now*, 71% of seven- to ten-year-olds feared that they might get stabbed or shot at school or at home. 70% feared that they might be hit by an adult. Neighborhoods have been disrupted by crime and social engineering. The main response of our policies has been to transfer childcare from home and neighborhood settings to institutions designed for custodial, safety and educational purposes.

One such policy is found in the movement for daycare. The claim is that daycare centers are superior to parent care because they can take advantage of the latest innovations in education and child psychology. However professional segregation deprives them of the experiences that appear when people take responsibility for each other simply because they live in the same communities. In *Death and Life of Great American Cities,* Jane Jacobs suggested:

> The myth that playgrounds and grass and hired guards or supervisors are innately wholesome for children and that the city streets filled with ordinary people are innately evil for children, boils down to a deep contempt for ordinary people (and for children).

Many public aspects of our society and its environments are not fit for children. Usually this obvious fact is minimized because the interests of children are not important enough to influence our social conduct. Instead, we uphold the myth that we will *do anything for our children*. In truth, we are more like a society that will *do anything to our children*.

If our society respected its immature members, we would ensure the safety of children in their neighborhoods. We would support parents' efforts to rear their children rather than accepting and even promoting public influences that are harmful to children.

Ageism that Treats Children as Adults

Perhaps surprisingly, juvenile ageism is expressed when children are treated as adults. In 1981 in *The Hurried Child: Growing Up Too Fast Too Soon*, psychologist David Elkind called attention to our society's trend toward regarding childhood and adolescence as stages of life to be outgrown as rapidly as possible. The philosopher Michael McFall in *Licensing Parents: Family, State, and Child Maltreatment* details the ways in which adolescents are being treated as adults to their detriment today.

Prematurely Awarding Adult Responsibilities

By placing adult responsibilities on them prematurely, children are expected to be independent at the expense of their developmental needs. This occurs when children must adjust to adults' personal problems, work schedules and lifestyles. It occurs when children are expected to raise younger siblings. It also occurs when children are expected to perform like adults in school and in athletics at ever earlier ages.

In her book *Ready or Not: Why Treating Children as Small Adults Endangers their Future,* Kay Hymowitz exposes the fallacious belief that socializing children is a wrongful use of power and that children should develop on their own. This fallacy has been reinforced by writers such as Judith Harris who implied that parents are less important than peers in her book *The Nurture Assumption*. Peers do outweigh parents on fashions and attitudes, but parents are the dominant influences on character development. The presumption that children will socialize themselves is false. It treats them like adults before they have adult capacities.

A dramatic example of treating an adolescent as an adult occurred in the Netherlands in 2009. A Dutch court blocked would-be-record-breaking thirteen-year-old Laura Dekker from a two-year solo sailing trip around the world. Intervening at the request of child protective services, the court put her under temporary supervision for two months to determine if she could withstand the physical and emotional risks. The fact that a court would even consider the adventure means it was open to treating teenagers as adults.

Applying Punitive Adult Policies

Misbehaving children typically are met with punitive measures in line with a "get tough on crime" public approach to adult offenders. Recent decades have seen a trend toward reacting to the "children and youth crisis" with immediate zero-tolerance interventions. This view considers children as the cause of crises rather than their families, neighborhoods, schools and society. The emphasis is on "get tough" policies rather than society's failure to provide safe homes and neighborhoods or to model personal responsibility.

In *Framing Youth: 10 Myths about the Next Generation*, Mike Males noted that the deteriorating behavior of American grownups in both personal and social realms has led to youth becoming the target of displaced anxiety and fury. He said, "when America's elders screw up big time, expect them to trash the younger generation with a vengeance."

Strategies commonly used by schools are suspension, expulsion and zero-tolerance policies that are reactive to behavior rather than dealing with the underlying causes. They presume that if youth know about harsh punishments they will be less inclined to misbehave. Children and adolescents now are arrested and criminalized for behavior that once was dealt with by principals or guidance counselors. They are being shifted from the educational to the juvenile justice system. There they may well be passed on to the adult correctional system where they become hardened criminals. In fact, these adult-based punitive policies have the opposite effect. Rebellious children are behaving irrationally in our view as we overlook the fact that they live in struggling, confusing families. Many are attracted to antisocial gangs in spite of, and some because of, our punitive policies. The bigger the crime, the higher the status in gangs.

Requiring Children to Testify in Adult Courtrooms

Until the 1980s, sexually abused children were traumatized by having to testify in court. Eventually their immaturity and vulnerability were recognized, and appropriate interviewing technologies were developed. Despite this awareness, children still can be required to testify in court rooms.

A lawyer from the Los Angeles Chapter of the organization Victims of Child Abuse Legislation said, "They're always trying to throw away the

Bill of Rights to protect children." This statement opposed legislation that would recognize that children are not adults and need special consideration in legal matters. The implication was that the Bill of Rights applies to adults but not to children.

Treating Children and Adolescents as Independent Persons

Systems that serve children often treat them as freestanding persons. When they are not treated as dependent parts of a parent-child unit, interventions actually can harm them. Proof of this abounds when adolescents are treated as adults in juvenile and criminal courts.

The limitations of the juvenile justice system illustrate how systems designed to protect and help young persons have the opposite effect when they ignore their families. In the *In re Gault* ruling in 1967, the U.S. Supreme Court found it necessary to protect children from inappropriate placements away from home by courts. Even that decision can aggravate situations by focusing attention on procedural due process for minors as if they are not part of a child-parent unit. When this happens, children and their parents are further removed from appropriate help.

Adolescent Childbearing

As long ago as 1987, the Committee on Child Development Research and Public Policy of the National Research Council concluded that the lack of a coherent policy toward adolescent pregnancy and childbearing contributed to the magnitude and seriousness of the problem. The Committee found that adolescent parenthood is a handicap because it interferes with development and opportunities in life. The Committee emphasized postponing sexual intercourse until both males and females are capable of wise and responsible decisions.

Although the rate of adolescent childbirth has been decreasing, the numbers remain unacceptably high. At the present time, 2.6 million children have been born to mothers under the age of eighteen, roughly 145,000 each year. Over 234,000 babies were born to 18 and 19 year-olds in 2011. A significant proportion of the next generation that will need to cope with an ever more demanding and competitive society is being raised by adolescents with their parents or likely alone if they are over 18.

Solutions have been stymied because of the characteristics of adolescence and because many adolescents want to have babies. Finding solutions is a formidable task in our society that prizes personal privacy and individual freedom and that broadly interprets reproductive freedom.

Rather than modeling self-restraint, the media exposes American adolescents to the most self-defeating of all possible messages. Sexual intercourse often is depicted as an activity with little mention of its risks or responsibilities. Non-marital sex is portrayed as exciting. Little informs adolescents about the consequences of sexual activity or the realities of childrearing.

What's more, children see premarital sex, cohabitation and multiple sexual relationships among the adults they know, including their own parents. Few if any other societies exhibit a more confusing combination of permissiveness and prudishness. The mixed messages result in an adolescent childbirth rate from two to seven times that of comparable nations.

As it now stands, biological and social pressures encourage rather than discourage adolescent pregnancy. Since the brain doesn't fully mature until the third decade of life, the ability to procreate is present long before the cognitive, emotional and social maturity required for parenthood. The average onset of menses at twelve, earlier initiation of sexual intercourse and intense social and peer pressures abetted by commercial exploitation of sexuality are powerful forces that promote teen pregnancy.

Many adolescents are wishful thinkers. Their sense of invulnerability and their attraction to risk means they believe "it can't happen to me." This underlies the "I don't care about that now" attitude despite knowing that cigarettes, drugs, noise and steroids produce disease, addiction, deafness and a shorter life span. *Monitoring the Future* surveys conducted by the Survey Research Center at the University of Michigan from 2001 to 2004 illuminate this attitude. For 56% of high school seniors having a child outside of marriage was considered a worthwhile lifestyle or was thought not to affect anyone else.

Even more importantly, babies and young children need to be protected from these characteristics. Immaturity is inherent in adolescence and cannot be eliminated by persuasion or education. Adolescents need competent parents and a society that supports self-restraint. Yet those who are most likely to become pregnant are seldom exposed to values and experiences that reveal the disadvantages of adolescent childbirth. Even with that knowledge, a substantial number of adolescents ignore it.

Usually we direct solutions at adolescents as if they were independent persons. We advocate sex education, the availability of contraceptives, parenting training, supportive education, welfare payments and expanded health care. None of those measures keep personal, educational, occupational and developmental opportunities from disappearing. We cannot expect family-life education, school-based health clinics and "increased life options" programs to change sexual behaviors and attitudes acquired through developmentally inappropriate sexual socialization or sexual abuse.

Our society's failure to deal with adolescent childbirth actually is a type of sexism against females, ageism against adolescents and racism against minorities. The combined force of this prejudice and discrimination is seen most poignantly with the black adolescent girl whose disadvantaged status is perpetuated when she is 1) impregnated to prove a "player's" masculinity (sexism); 2) deprived of the opportunity to complete her adolescent development (juvenile ageism); and 3) publically viewed as following her cultural heritage and destiny (racism).

If we truly wish to prevent adolescent pregnancies and childbirth, we need to recognize that developmental characteristics and parental influences, or the lack thereof, are more important than ignorance and socioeconomic disadvantage. Antipoverty measures alone won't address key parent-child relationship problems. Ronald Mincy and Susan Weiner of the Urban Institute found that poverty is less important than the parents in an adolescent girl's chances of becoming pregnant.

The focus also needs to extend to boys and young men. As long as boys fail to postpone fatherhood until they have steady employment and as long as men do not support their children, mothers and children will remain trapped in poor neighborhoods where social problems incubate and human services are ineffective.

Unfortunately, efforts to reduce adolescent pregnancy encounter powerful resistances. One is the belief that public attitudes toward irresponsible sexual behavior cannot be changed. Therefore, when pregnancy occurs, the focus is on pregnancy termination or on supporting the adolescent during pregnancy and while raising the child. Heated arguments revolve around notifying an adolescent's parents about the pregnancy as well as termination. Seldom are questions raised about the adolescents' ability to make life-altering decisions or their ability to rear children. Another resistance arises from the emphasis on a fetus's right to life that does not include the fetus's right to competent parents after birth.

Our society cannot afford to shortchange the nurturing and protection of its immature members by allowing them to assume adult responsibilities. If we define parenthood as an adult responsibility, we can restore adolescence as a developmental stage of life for pregnant adolescents.

AGEISM IN SERVICES FOR CHILDREN

When managing the lives of children is turned over to impersonal institutions, adverse consequences can result. Institutions have considerations that might not reflect the interests of the children they serve.

Social service, correctional, legal and mental health institutions occupy established slots in our economy. They are as dependent on their clients as their clients are upon them. This does not mean that professionals intend to promote the continuation of the problems they are supposed to solve. But institutional factors like the lack of interagency collaboration, budget cuts and protecting budgetary turfs can stall them at the level of servicing rather than solving economic, social and family problems.

Policies and practices reflect inadvertent juvenile ageism when children are treated impersonally and categorically. For example, two blanket social services policies override the interests of individual children. The first is the child protection policy that removes children from abusive parents. When the child removal policy dominates, children can be taken from their homes and placed in foster care indefinitely. The conditions that led to their removal may never be addressed effectively. The second is the family preservation policy meant to maintain existing family structures. Because of the shortage of effective services and the failure to follow statutory requirements, this policy can keep children in, and return children to, families that further damage them. Instead of adhering to blanket policies, the needs of each child and family should determine how best to help that child.

Similarly, public schools have long been used to achieve sociopolitical aims such as crime prevention, poverty amelioration and racial integration. Each goal might be laudable but each one can deflect attention from the developmental needs of the young and the vital role of parent-child relationships in those social problems.

What's more, services meant to benefit children can serve the interests of those who provide them instead. For example, the primary role of childcare systems is to serve the adults who delegate childcare to others and those who provide the childcare rather than the interests of the children themselves.

Another example can be found in federal regulations that mandate costly treatment for every newborn not born dead. This is done without regard for the newborn's quality of life or the baby's family. No financial provisions are provided once these severely handicapped, technologically dependent babies leave neonatal intensive care. Since their families are financially and emotionally stressed and the children do not have a fully conscious life, the quality of their families' lives, including that of their siblings, is grossly impaired.

AGEISM IN CHILD DEVELOPMENT RESEARCH

As David Hamburg, Executive Director of the Carnegie Foundation, pointed out in *The Family Crucible and Healthy Child Development*, newborns in the United States are treated like experimental subjects. We expose them to an unlimited variety of parents until they are damaged by neglect and abuse. Then we study them to see what kind of parenting they had.

More specifically, the way questions are framed in child development research can reflect juvenile ageism. This prejudice underlies resiliency research that assesses how much neglect and abuse or how much placement in non-familial environments young children can tolerate without being permanently damaged. Compare this to research on how much neglect and abuse or how much segregation Jews, blacks or elders could tolerate without being seriously damaged to bring the prejudice into clear view.

Research on child neglect and abuse usually asks whether actions and practices harm children rather than whether they are in the developmental interests of children. Even though adult women are readily designated as victims of domestic abuse on the basis of their complaints, children often are not considered victims of abuse unless they are obviously damaged by it. Instead of assuming that they need competent parents, the assumption is that they aren't harmed by their parents unless serious damage can be proved. The research therefore focuses on the resilience of neglected and abused children rather than on the children's developmental interests in the quality of their parenting.

In a similar vein, research on the effects of parental prenatal substance abuse assesses the extent of damage to children later in life. The ongoing *Maternal Lifestyle Study* conducted at four NICHD Neonatal Research Network sites found in 2008 that the damage is less than previously thought. Along with declining rates of adolescent pregnancy and alcohol and substance abuse, these findings are used to reduce the importance of these problems as if there is an acceptable level of damage to children.

Other studies are similarly flawed. Research on the effects of childcare on children usually takes for granted the unavailability of parents employed away from home and doesn't ask how much non-parental care is in the developmental interests of the children or the parents. Criminology research focuses on children as offenders—delinquents—rather than as victims of adversity.

When the emphasis of research is on assessing how much children are harmed by incompetent parents, maternal prenatal drug use and separation from their parents, a child's need for competent parents is not taken into account.

WHEN PUBLIC PROGRAMS PLACE PARENTAL WISHES ABOVE CHILDREN'S INTERESTS

The following article in the *Tampa Bay Times* about the work of a Florida task force devoted to "helping babies in drug withdrawal" through Neonatal Abstinence exemplifies the way in which a narrow focus on a specific problem obscures the big picture and results in continuing newborn babies in circumstances that are contrary to their interests:

> *Sarah Ryan had previously lost custody of her three sons in the context of her long-standing battle with drug addiction. When she became pregnant again she was "petrified to actually tell a physician that I was addicted, because I didn't want to lose my child." She finally did tell her doctor and was put on methadone during the last trimester of*

pregnancy. When born her baby Quinn seemed healthy, but on his third day he began to show signs of methadone withdrawal. He was placed on methadone and then weaned over 3 ½ weeks in intensive care. Ryan now is caring for her healthy baby and receiving treatment through the Tampa Drug Abuse Comprehensive Coordinating Office.

In this example the narrow focus on the wishes of a mother and on the condition of a newborn baby completely ignored the fact that this mother had been found to be an unfit parent for three previous children. Instead of seeking a pre-emptive termination of parental rights based on her history and the fact of neonatal child abuse through the use of drugs the point was that *more research is called for to identify the best way to treat newborns in withdrawal.* The goal of the task force is "not to arrest mothers and take their babies away from mothers. It's to prevent this (babies in drug withdrawal) from happening." It is not a stretch to see this attitude as deferring to the wishes of mothers and viewing their newborn babies as their property rather than as persons with rights and interests of their own...as an expression of juvenile ageism.

WHERE ARE WE?

In all of these systems that presumably are intended to help our young people, the failure of professionals and their funders to make corrections in policies and practices in the face of demonstrated harm to young people makes inadvertent juvenile ageism more sinister. A prominent example is found in the "war against child abuse." In some respects, it has become a war against children who become its casualties when they are treated solely as individuals rather than as part of a child/parent unit in a family that is crying out for help. This brings us to the ways in which juvenile ageism harms our young citizens.

Chapter Seven

The Impact of Juvenile Ageism on Individuals

*We are always too busy for our children. We never give them
the time or interest they deserve. We lavish gifts upon them,
but the most precious gift—our personal association, which
means so much to them—we give grudgingly and throw it
away on those who care for it so little.*

MARK TWAIN

Ageism against an individual child disregards that child as a person with
moral and civil rights. The most extreme form is seen in the belief that
parents own their children like property. This was reflected in a letter cir-
culated by the National Parents' Survey on Public Education:

> Dear Friend:
>
> Who owns your children?
> Who decides what values, attitudes, and beliefs they should
> hold?
> Is it you—the parent?
> Or is it government through the public education system?

CHILDREN AS PROPERTY

The belief that children are the property of their parents draws upon the deeply ingrained assumption that genetic parents have natural affection for their offspring and that parenthood is a reproductive right. It is supported by the legal presumption that others can interfere with parental authority only when parents seriously damage children through neglect or abuse.

There is another side of this coin. The ambivalent emotions inherent in all parent-child relationships are depicted in the Oedipus complex. In Sophocles' tragedy *Oedipus Rex,* his mother Jocasta arranges to have three-day-old Oedipus killed because she fears he will ultimately kill her husband. As an adult, Oedipus discovers this from a servant:

> OEDIPUS: You mean she gave the child to you?
> SERVANT: Yes, my lord.
> OEDIPUS: Why did she do that?
> SERVANT: So I would kill it.
> OEDIPUS: That wretched woman (his wife) was the mother?
> SERVANT: Yes. She was afraid of dreadful prophecies.
> OEDIPUS: What sort of prophecies?
> SERVANT: The story went that he would kill his father.

After this revelation, Jocasta commits suicide and Oedipus, who has mistakenly married his mother and killed his father, blinds himself and becomes homeless. Both mother and son suffer from their beliefs and actions. Sophocles dramatically calls attention to the conflicting feelings, motives and actions naturally involved to a less intense degree in parent-child relationships. This ambivalence is fertile soil for prejudice and discrimination when children are regarded as their parents' property.

At the deepest psychological levels, we cannot overlook the tradition of parents having total control over their children's lives…even the ability to abandon and kill them, as still is done in some parts of the world. The Biblical example of Abraham and Isaac illustrates the power of a parent over a child. Although the practice of child sacrifice was abandoned long ago, it continues to exert a powerful unconscious influence. The following examples demonstrate how this absolute control persists.

Killing a Child is Not Murder

Homicide is the leading cause of death by injury for babies in the United States. Michael Petit, President of Every Child Matters, pointed out in 2011 that over the previous 10 years, more than 20,000 American children are believed to have been killed in their own homes by family members. That is nearly four times the number of U.S. soldiers killed in Iraq and Afghanistan during that time. The child maltreatment death rate in the U.S. is triple Canada's and 11 times that of Italy. This number is low because between 60% and 85% of child fatalities due to maltreatment are not recorded as such on death certificates.

In New York City, a mother's drug abuse caused the premature birth and death of her child; the death was ruled as "natural causes." In Indiana, murder charges against Melody Baldwin were dropped when she pleaded guilty to child abuse after administering a fatal dose of a drug to her four-year-old son. In Wisconsin, a judge remarked that the death by beating of a twenty-month-old boy by his twenty-six-year-old prostitute mother "may well have been a benevolent grace for the child" because of the sordid life that boy would otherwise have had to bear.

A more subtle but revealing sign of juvenile ageism is found in a New York City Child Fatality Report. Generally the deaths of premature newborns caused by their mothers' drug abuse were noted as "deaths from natural causes."

Our society has a deep-seated respect for the mother-child relationship along with an understandable aversion to blaming parents. This is best illustrated by the public reaction that any mother who kills her children must be mentally ill.

> A 29-year-old mother, Kimberly Martin, was charged with first degree murder in the deaths of 8-year-old Dusty and 4-year-old Brandy, whose bodies were found in her car when she was stopped for speeding in Council Bluffs, Iowa. Each child was shot in the head. The insanity of a mother who shot and killed her two young children appeared so clear-cut that neither the prosecution nor the judge required evidence that Martin was mentally ill at the time of the shootings. The judge found

Kimberly Martin innocent by reason of insanity and released her from custody.

The fact that the victims were her own children allowed Martin's murders to be explained in a way that would be unacceptable if she had murdered two adults. With the murder of adults determining innocence by reason of insanity involves questions about premeditation, awareness of right and wrong and the ability to adhere to the right. These questions used to determine insanity were not raised in Martin's case. The verdict also presumes that murdering her own children doesn't suggest that she might be dangerous to others as well.

What if Dusty and Brandy Martin had been killed by their father or a different relative? We can't escape the possibility that the tradition of a child as a mother's property lies in the background of this and similar cases. The reluctance to believe that a mother could intentionally harm her child further confuses the issue. Latent guilt in those of us who are parents also could encourage us to deny the guilt of other parents.

The following note left by a mother who killed her daughter in St. Petersburg, Florida, before killing herself reveals the self-centered side of motherly love:

> I couldn't even take care of my daughter. I had to take her with me. I had no choice. I would not want her to go through her life without me in it.

Killing an Abusive Parent is Murder

Killing your own parent can't be excused under any circumstances. Still, a parent's superior power can goad a helpless, damaged child into the understandable response of attacking the abuser. Studies of adolescents who killed their parents reveal that many acted in self-defense. All of them released pent-up rage instilled by years of being battered. Slaves responded in similar ways to abusive masters.

Nevertheless, parricide is treated as murder by a society that ignores child maltreatment until it becomes publicly visible. Both parents and society contribute to juvenile ageism. In the words of Terry Adams, a teen who shot his physically and emotionally abusive alcoholic father and mother:

> The biggest thing is just being aware. Care, 'cause if you don't, it's not just the little kid you are hurting, you're hurting tomorrow.... Because kids are defenseless, they don't have the vocabulary, the mental capacity, the mentality, the strong points to stand up. If someone won't stand up for them, nobody will. If no one does, then, what's tomorrow?

The view that parents who are killed by their children are victims while the victim status of their children is ignored betrays a prejudice against children. Of course, many adult murderers were neglected and abused as children. It's not that their crimes don't warrant prosecution. It's that as childhood victims of neglect and abuse our society didn't value them enough to ensure adequate care for them. Thus, parents can be seen as victims of the children they have victimized. A society that accepts this formulation clearly discriminates against its young.

Exploitation of a Child

Children are particularly vulnerable to prejudice and discrimination in their own homes. They compete with their parents for time, money, attention and affection. They require compromise and sacrifice of adult wishes and needs. In response, many parents neglect their children or take out their frustrations on them. When children adapt to neglect or abuse, they are considered resilient.

> Katie Beers was called "the cockroach kid" in her neighborhood. At the age of 6, she was on the streets from dawn to darkness cutting her first-grade classes regularly. She survived as a Dickens street waif in a modern strip mall. At the age of 10, she came to the attention of authorities when she was found in a secret room underneath a Bay Shore home where she had been kept a prisoner by a family friend John Esposito. After closely reviewing their files, county social service officials believe they had handled the case properly before this discovery.

Suffolk county Court Judge Joel Lefkowitz sentenced Esposito to a 15 years to life prison sentence for kidnapping. He also sentenced Sal Inghilleri, the husband of Katie's godmother, to a 14-year prison for sexually abusing Katie, saying Inghilleri had "robbed her of her youth."

The media coverage—forty articles in *Newsday*—portrayed Katie as a heroic figure, even a celebrity. She showed the qualities admired in adults... perseverance, adaptability and an uncomplaining attitude that enabled her to surmount adversity. Her premature adulthood was seen as a virtue rather than as a defense against maltreatment. This view shifted attention away from the adults who mistreated her. The impact of interrupting her education, missing unencumbered play with peers and future effects on her personality and social development was completely ignored.

Most significantly, depriving a child of the opportunity to live childhood as a developmental stage wasn't seen as the same as depriving adults of opportunities to fulfill their potential. Katie Beers was a victim of prejudice and discrimination by caretakers and a society that treats children as less important than adults. She was enslaved by parent figures, neglected by educational and social services and unprotected by society. In the end, she became a heroine, not a victim. This defensive distortion occurs regularly when survivors of child maltreatment are portrayed as heroic figures while attention is deflected away from their cruel treatment. Adults under the same circumstances would be considered victims of oppression and possibly torture who display the Stockholm Syndrome.

In the movie *Precious,* an obese, poor, illiterate, young black woman who was sexually and emotionally abused becomes a heroine. A public relations specialist in Manhattan found it a "deeply moving way to show the beauty and innocence of a poor, fat, dark-skinned woman. At the end of the film, Precious looked angelic to me."

The Fetus is a Mother's Property

There has been a long-standing legal tendency to regard an unborn child as part of the mother's body and therefore as her property. The limits of this belief were clarified in 1973 by the U.S. Supreme Court ruling in *Roe v. Wade* that recognized the rights of a woman over the rights of the fetus during the first trimester, of the fetus over the mother in the second and third trimesters and of a physician throughout pregnancy to make decisions regarding its termination.

The specification of maternal and fetal rights during pregnancy caused an abortion controversy that the U.S. Supreme Court returned to state legislatures in *Webster v. Reproductive Health Services* in 1989. Because of this, the definition of ageism against a fetus remains to be clarified as our society defines its stand on abortion. In the medical community, the trend toward recognizing both the mother and an older fetus as separate patients has been prompted by surgery on a late-term fetus.

Sympathy Obscures Incompetence

The case of seventeen-year-old Jamine Bedwell illustrates how sympathy for an adolescent mother can obscure her parental incompetence even when it results in her baby's murder. The headline of one newspaper article was: "Mother Did Her Best for Infant: Officials Say the Teen Mother Tried to Keep Her Son Safe, But Could Not Stop Her Abusive Boyfriend."

> Jasmine Bedwell's ex-boyfriend, 21-year-old Richard McTear, attacked her, drove off, and threw her baby Emanuel on to an interstate highway. Caught a few hours later, he was jailed facing 10 charges, including first-degree murder.
>
> Tampa police records show Bedwell ran away from home at least 21 times. She was arrested 10 times, including a battery charge at the age of 11. Social workers intervened when she was 14. At 17, she gave birth to Emanuel. The father, Emanuel Murray, 22, was soon out of the picture, imprisoned on weapons charges.
>
> McTear's record was filled with domestic violence arrests. McTear's beatings sent Bedwell to the hospital, according to a Department of Children and Families report. She went to court with a case worker to obtain an injunction against McTear whom process servers could not find. After 15 days, Bedwell did not pick up required paperwork. She did not attend a hearing

several days later nor did McTear, who returned to her home to assault her and murder her baby.

Jeff Rainey, president and CEO of Hillsborough Kids Inc., a privately contracted child support service, said Bedwell did everything she could to protect Emanuel.

The focus on the older man who repeatedly abused Bedwell and on her statement "I love my baby with all my heart, and he was the only thing I had left in life" ignores the fact that a baby was killed because of her ineptness as an adolescent. Emanuel's right to life was obscured. The support given to a troubled girl because she said she loved her baby despite the fact that her actions and inactions proved otherwise reflects two kinds of juvenile ageism. The first treats adolescents as adults. The second treats babies as objects whose only purpose is to fulfill their parents' needs.

The Baby Business

Parents across time have weighed the eventual economic contribution of their children in the rice field or the manor against the cost of childhood. They have used infanticide or abandonment to rid themselves of less-valued offspring. They also have sold them into slavery or indentured servitude.

Over the last thirty years, advances in reproductive medicine have created another market for babies. Affluent parents choose traits, clinics woo clients and specialized providers earn millions of dollars a year. The typical costs of sperm are $300; eggs $4,500; *in vitro* fertilization $67,000 to $114,000 per live birth; surrogacy $59,000; adoption $2,500 for a foster child, $15,000 for a domestic baby and $25,000 for an international child; and pre-implantation genetic diagnosis $3,500. Physicians, who might charge over $10,000 for a procedure, need to answer a series of thorny ethical, safety and social welfare questions.

Because few want to define baby-making as a business, and because the endeavor touches deeply on the most difficult moral dilemmas, many governments have either ignored this trade in children or simply prohibited it. An exception is that since 1991 the United Kingdom Human Fertilization and Embryology Authority has adopted rules for *in vitro* fertilization and embryo manipulation. In the United States, no binding rules deter a private clinic from offering a menu of sperm and egg traits or from implanting women with embryos.

In all of these instances, sperm, eggs, embryos and fetuses are treated as commodities to be manipulated, bought and sold without considering the consequences for the product…a human being. Technology is forcing the legal system to define the fundamental meaning of parents, of a family and of reproduction. It must consider current structures and develop new policy options for the marketplace: recipients, donors and children as well as the industry that serves them.

In another vein in 2004, when Playtex débuted a breast pump called Embrace, no one pointed out that something you plug into a wall socket is a far cry from cuddling and a kiss. Pumps are a handy way to avoid the privately agonizing and publicly unpalatable question: Does the mother or her milk matter more to the baby? Many of breast-feeding's benefits come from the cuddling that accompanies it. The stark difference between employer-sponsored lactation programs and flesh-and-blood family life is difficult to overstate. Some lactation rooms even "ban babies lest mothers smuggle them in for a quick nip."

Irresponsible Artificial Fertilization

Some women choose to not have babies. Others exhaust every option to have a baby after they've been told they cannot have one. Since the birth of the world's first "test-tube baby," Louise Brown in July 1978, the world has seen an estimated 5 million babies resulting from IVF and other assisted reproductive technologies, according to a presentation at the 2012 International Committee for Monitoring Assisted Reproductive Technologies.

Arthur Caplan, bioethics chairman at the University of Pennsylvania, notes that not enough attention is paid to the wellbeing of the children in IVF multiple births. Everyone has a stake in high-multiple births. They cause insurance premiums to rise when hospitals are not reimbursed properly. Those with disabilities typically require medical and social services.

"To say all you need is cash and the will to have more kids should not be a sufficient standard to access fertility services," Caplan said. "It's insufficient for adoption. It isn't sufficient to be a foster parent. Why would it be sufficient to run down to the fertility clinic to get embryos transplanted or super-ovulated?"

> Nadya Suleman, a 33-year-old single mother, already had six children, ages 2 to 7, when she gave birth to octuplets on January 26, 2009. She had all 14 of her children through *in vitro* fertilization. She had been supporting herself in part on the more than $165,000 in disability payments she collected for a work injury and from $490 a month in food stamps. She had suffered bouts of paranoia and depression.

> Suleman told NBC's *Today* she never stopped trying to get pregnant by fertility treatment to extend her family and make up for being an only child. "That was always a dream of mine, to have a large family, a huge family." She said that her childhood left her feeling a lack of self and identity. She was deluged with offers for book deals, TV shows, and other business proposals.

Raina Kelley, a *Newsweek* reporter, commented about what the outrage over Suleman says about our society.

> We created Octomom. Our democracy gives people the right to have as many children as they want. With our glorification of bizarre behavior, we dare the emotionally needy to shock and appall us. Then we slam them.

Fetal Damage is Not the Responsibility of the Parent

In most states, whether a pregnant person's drug abuse constitutes child abuse is an open question. Still some prosecutors, judges and child-protection workers say they have an obligation to protect fetuses. The district attorney of California's Butte County vowed to seek jail terms for pregnant women who refuse to obtain treatment for drug abuse. Others say such action would create fetal rights that have no foundation in law.

In 1991, the Michigan Court of Appeals ruled that Kimberly Hardy, a twenty-four-year-old factory worker, should not stand trial on child abuse charges for using crack hours before her son's birth. The child abuse statute did not apply to fetuses. On the other hand, in Westchester County, New

York, a drug-abusing woman lost custody of her baby at birth after a judge ruled the child was likely to be neglected after birth.

In another case in Washington, D.C., twenty-nine-year-old Brenda Vaughn pleaded guilty to forgery. Because tests showed that she had used cocaine, the Superior Court in the District of Columbia sent her to jail until her due date to protect the fetus from drug abuse. That case kindled heated debate about the use of child abuse and drug laws to prosecute illegal drug users and to place their newborns in foster care. Efforts to incarcerate pregnant drug addicts to prevent fetal damage have been criticized. The concern is that if a woman can be arrested for endangering a fetus with cocaine, she might be arrested for drinking alcohol or smoking. The failure to tie damage suffered by a fetus caused by the mother's behavior to a child's later disabilities clearly reflects juvenile ageism.

Parental Abduction

The kidnapping of children by their parents is another example of children being regarded as possessions. Although the interests of children might be served by parental abduction at times, the most common cause is parents retaliating against each other.

Family violence might be involved in parental abduction. The abductor might be the violent one or the one fleeing violence. In other instances of abduction, parents ease their emotional pain despite the pain it causes the other parent or the confusion and stress experienced by the children. In any event, a child is being treated like an object to be possessed.

Removal from Adoptive Parents

Ageism exists when children's interests are disregarded by removing them from adoptive parents and returning them to incompetent genetic parents because of technical or legal errors in the adoption process. The child is treated as an object that can be readily moved from one place to another rather than as a human being with developmental needs and legal rights.

The case of *In the Interests of J. L. W.* is an example. In Wisconsin, a five-month-old boy was abandoned by his mother. When he was eighteen months, parental rights were terminated so he could be adopted by an aunt and uncle. Two years later, the state Supreme Court returned him to his genetic mother because of a technical error in the adoption rather than considering the child's circumstances and developmental interests in a new trial. The Court's order treated the child as an object and took him away from the only parents he knew.

In New Haven, Connecticut, a one-year-old girl was returned to the nineteen-year-old mother who had abandoned her at birth. Five months after the termination of her parental rights, the mother asked to have her child returned. After legal action, the child was returned to her genetic mother without considering her attachment bonds with her adoptive parents, the only parents she knew.

In these cases technical procedural issues forced the return of children to unfit parents. But when the legal issue actually hinges on genetic or psychological relationships between parents and children, the psychological relationship usually is considered paramount. In 1983, in *Lehr v. Robertson,* the U.S. Supreme Court held that the emotional attachment, not the genetic relationship, defines the family.

Retrieval of Switched Baby

The belief that a child is the property of the genetic parents is further illustrated by the usual response to babies who are switched at birth. A Sarasota, Florida, couple tried to determine if their deceased nine-year-old daughter had been mistakenly switched at birth with another nine-year-old named Kimberly Mays. They never considered the adverse effect such a pursuit might have on the living child. After one court granted them visitation rights on the basis of genetic testing, Kimberly fortunately was able to obtain a "divorce" from them in another court.

Corporal Punishment

Controversy over corporal punishment hinges on the fact that, although it is prohibited in many states' public schools, it has not been deemed by the U.S. Supreme Court to be cruel and unusual punishment. Some people advocate corporal punishment because it is consistent with Biblical teachings. Others see any form of physical intervention as child abuse and the promotion of violence.

Those who advocate corporal punishment can use their beliefs to disguise child abuse. They might be reliving the violence they faced early in their lives. Those who oppose corporal punishment can use their beliefs to deprive children of useful lessons about the consequences of their behavior. Juvenile ageism is evidenced in both extremes. Realistic developmental interests are ignored when adults base their behavior on ideological beliefs rather than on the circumstances in which physical interventions are appropriate in the course of childrearing.

ANIMAL PROTECTION HAS A HIGHER PRIORITY

The way we protect animals contrasts with the way we protect children. A specific example is the handling of sea lions at Pier 39 in San Francisco, California. The same year that seven-year-old Katie Beers hauled her family's dirty clothes to a laundromat, a group of sea lions began hauling out on K-dock. The outpouring of protection and support provided to the sea lions by that community then stood in sharp contrast with the community neglect of Katie.

Over 135 years of "child saving" has done little to reduce child neglect and abuse in the United States. The prevention of cruelty to animals, however, has been so successful that public protests against the use of animals in medical research are readily organized. Significantly, the formation of the New York Society for the Prevention of Cruelty to Children was preceded by a decade by the New York Society for the Prevention of Cruelty to Animals.

RESPONSES OF THE YOUNG TO JUVENILE AGEISM

When young people internalize juvenile ageism, they often question their legitimacy, doubt their abilities and perpetuate a culture of silence. They feel that they really don't count. They seek the approval of adults even if it means betraying other children by tattling on siblings or becoming the teacher's pet.

In a positive vein, discrimination against the young is increasingly recognized as bigotry around the world. The 2009 Portland National Youth Summit drafted a *Mental Health Youth Bill of Rights*. An increasing number of social institutions are acknowledging children and youth as an oppressed minority group, especially when adolescents are generally characterized as immature, violent and rebellious.

Psychotherapists, juvenile probation personnel, teachers and other helping persons have a special responsibility to avoid juvenile ageism by viewing young people as citizens with a right to participate in, and a responsibility to serve, their communities. Proponents of building on the strengths of young people through youth-adult partnerships and healthier communities offer a contrast to the view of the young as societal burdens that need to be controlled.

Curricula are available for educating adults about juvenile ageism. Organizations responding to the negative effects of juvenile ageism, including the United Nations in its Convention on the Rights of the Child (Articles 5 and 12), Human Rights Watch, the National Youth Rights Association, Youth on Board and the Free Child Project, envision a world where young people are fully respected and treated as valued, active members of their families, communities and society.

Establishing and cultivating a productive, positive social climate requires adults and youth to take stock of their current beliefs. Adults need to exercise leadership roles in a spirit of service and respect especially when dealing with disrespectful youth. Young people need encouragement to assume responsibility for their own behavior and for learning.

LACK OF AWARENESS OF JUVENILE AGEISM

One reason why the elderly are more readily seen as victims of ageism than children is that most of us do not encounter egregious forms of juvenile ageism. We support public schools and child-oriented charities while deploring child neglect and abuse. Most children are valued and well-treated.

Our lack of awareness is understandable. First of all, juvenile ageism is eclipsed by our concern about racism and sexism. Second, we all are juvenile ageists to some degree. Third, we all have difficulty recognizing our prejudices even when they are pointed out to us. As much as we might like to believe otherwise, all of our judgments are biased by our experiences and our emotional states.

Juvenile ageism and other prejudices are easily obscured because they can be expressed in benevolent ways. Prejudice as an attitude and discrimination as a behavior are easier to recognize when they are expressed in malevolent ways. When children are oppressed, abused and neglected, it's easier to accept the existence of juvenile ageism than when we believe we are helping and protecting them.

Making the case for juvenile ageism is a difficult task. In some ways, to speak of juvenile ageism now is like speaking about racism in Atlanta, Georgia, in the 1850s. The economic interests and latent guilt of plantation owners kept them from recognizing slavery as a racist institution. Today, the latent guilt of adults and the commercial exploitation of the young keep us from recognizing juvenile ageism in our society and in our families.

WHAT DOES ALL OF THIS MEAN?

Because prejudice and discrimination are inherent in the human condition, active efforts are required to combat them. The concept of juvenile ageism helps us become aware that attitudes toward children can be prejudiced and that behavior toward children can be discriminatory. Juvenile ageism can be easily equated with elder ageism. Neglecting the interests of children because they are less important than and are inferior to adults is the same as neglecting the interests of persons whose race or gender is seen as relegating them to an inferior status.

Juvenile ageism has the virulence of racism and the prevalence of sexism. It fosters the belief that parents can create and rear children without facing responsibilities to them or to society. It enables the exploitation, neglect, abuse, abduction and even murder of children. It has contributed to the alienation of our youth from society's positive values. It is the greatest barrier to recognizing the interests of our young citizens in our political processes, in services for children and adolescents and in households.

The consequences of juvenile ageism are a political system that fails to create safe environments for children; a commercial system that exploits the young; social services that are overwhelmed by child neglect and abuse cases; an impaired workforce; and a fragile economy. It has resulted in staggering costs from violence, habitual crime and welfare dependency...the ultimate products of child neglect and abuse.

Identifying and overcoming juvenile ageism requires a civil rights approach. If you feel hopeless about confronting or defeating juvenile ageism, you are confirming the ingrained power of this prejudice. Children should be recognized as citizens from birth. This means sensitizing the public to the existence of juvenile ageism and to the developmental requirements of childhood and adolescence.

Beyond that is the need for advocacy for newborns, children and adolescents as well as their families. Of greatest importance is respect and support for the responsibilities of parenthood. Short-term sacrifices for long-term gain are politically unpopular in a society devoted to immediate gratification. Yet the direct benefits to adults of a society in which children can thrive are reductions in crime, safe streets, integrity in commerce and politics, wholesome environments and economic prosperity.

Overcoming juvenile ageism will benefit all adults and the next generation. Because it involves protecting our young and planning for the future, it's a theme around which improving our entire society can be organized. The immediate question is should we continue to expect children to cope with the stressors our society imposes on them? Ageism makes children responsible for coping with adult failings. Instead, we should minimize avoidable stressors for children and adolescents. This would emphasize our society's responsibility to protect and nurture our young citizens...our next generation.

If juvenile ageism is not addressed, our nation is in peril. The emphasis will continue to fall on parents to protect their children from its hostile, exploitative elements rather than on creating a benevolent society that values its young and its own future. The first challenge is to recognize and protect the rights and developmental needs of our newborn babies and young children.

Chapter Eight

The Rights and Needs of Newborn Babies and Young Children

There is no such thing as a baby... A baby cannot exist alone but is essentially part of a relationship.

D.W. WINNICOTT, PEDIATRICIAN
THE CHILD, THE FAMILY, AND THE OUTSIDE WORLD

Significant strides have been made to overcome blatant juvenile ageism even though it has not been formally acknowledged as a form of prejudice and discrimination. Childhood and adolescence are recognized as unique stages of development today. Still, the fact that a newborn baby is a unique human being—and a citizen—isn't recognized in popular thought or most legal doctrines. This isn't surprising. It took a long time for older children to gain recognition as human beings with basic rights.

Seeing a child as immature rather than as merely ignorant took shape in the Eighteenth Century. Rousseau and the Romantic poets dispelled the distorted view that children are miniature adults. The Civil War established the civil rights of individual adults and created the opportunity for a vision of the civil rights of children and the role of the state in American life.

In 1870 the Illinois Supreme Court decision in *People v. Turner* extended due process protection to minors. It set the stage for juvenile courts that were established in 1899 and expanded in the 1910s to administer payments to single mothers, a precursor of the contemporary federal Temporary Assistance for Needy Families program.

A wide-ranging "save the children" movement ushered in the Twentieth Century as the Century of the Child. The New York Society for the Prevention of Cruelty to Children had been formed in 1875. In 1900 the Swedish feminist Ellen Key published *The Century of the Child*. In her vision, babies would be conceived by loving parents. They would grow up in homes where mothers were ever-present.

This vision dominated most of the first half of the 1900s. The aim was to map out a childhood in which children would acquire the "habit of happiness." This inspired the professional approach to childhood and adolescence through pediatrics, developmental psychology, child-centered education, child welfare, child and adolescent psychology and psychiatry and policy studies related to the young.

In the second half of the Twentieth Century, a sense arose that childhood was disappearing. The worlds of children and adults were merging again. Materially better off than sixty years ago, children are often being expected now to be independent and to adjust to a variety of family styles. Adolescents especially are wooed as major consumers. The more children act like adults in sports and in schools, the better.

Underlying these developments is recognition of the rights of minors. These rights culminate in most adult legal rights being granted typically at the age of 18 during late adolescence. Eligibility for these rights presumably begins at birth.

The Rights of Children

Rights have two distinct but related functions: to protect a person's freedoms and to fill important needs. The most important needs of children are protection from harm by others and themselves and to grow up to become productive citizens.

Minors lack the capacity and experience to marry, enter contracts and bring lawsuits without adult guidance. They are considered minors until they reach the age of majority at either 18 or 21, depending upon the state and the privileges. Until then, they are required to have legal and physical custodians, usually their parents. Since late adolescents are older than 18 and are regarded as legal adults in most ways, references to adolescent rights in this Chapter are limited to early and middle adolescence.

When newborn babies and children were regarded as property, they had no rights. Only their parents had rights based on the liberties and privacy of individuals. Now those parental rights are legal (acting on behalf of) and custodial (residential). Over the last century, minors have been accorded a series of moral and civil rights based on moral and civil rights that apply to all human beings.

The Moral Rights of Minors

Moral rights reflect cultural values devoted to the common good and compassion for others. Emmanuel Kant said that each human being "must always be treated as an end, not merely as a means." To treat another person as a means is to use that person to advance one's own interests. To treat another person as an end is to respect that person's dignity and autonomy. This distinction is especially important for young persons who are vulnerable to oppression and exploitation.

The traditional caretaker view of minor's moral rights was articulated in 1691 by the philosopher John Locke. According to him, all humans are "born infants, weak and helpless, without knowledge or understanding." Therefore, parents were "by the law of nature under an obligation to preserve, nourish, and educate the children they had begotten." In Locke's scheme, parents have the right to make choices for their children:

> Whilst [the child] is in an estate wherein he has no understanding of his own to direct his will, he is not to have any will of his own to follow.

Moral rights impose a duty to actively help a person. For example, a minor's moral right to education imposes a duty to provide that education.

Eglantyne Jebb, founder of the Save the Children Fund, began an effort to codify the moral rights of minors in 1922 in England's Charter of the Rights of the Child. The Charter spelled out the moral right of all minors to be protected from exploitation; to be given a chance for full physical, mental and moral development; and to be taught to live a life of service. The League of Nations adopted the charter in 1924 as the Geneva Declaration of the Rights of the Child.

In the United States, the moral rights of minors have been detailed in a variety of organizational creeds, children's bills of rights and White House Conferences on Children. Further declarations have come from the United Nations. These rights reflect reasonable expectations that minors will be given whatever they require to grow into healthy, functional adults. The United Nations Convention on the Rights of the Child states that all human beings are born with the following inherent civil rights:

- to survival;

- to develop to the fullest;

- to protection from harmful influences, abuse and exploitation; and

- to participate fully in family, cultural and social life.

Whenever policymakers express their hopes for children, they effectively conclude that children have a moral right to competent parents... and specifically to not live in foster care or institutions. When parents and other persons make decisions for a child, they act as fiduciary custodians. They are expected to put themselves in the child's position and place the child's interests above their own. The contemporary challenge is to apply the same principles to newborn babies.

The Civil Rights of Minors

Moral rights are not enough to protect minors from abuse and neglect. For this reason, certain moral rights of minors have become legal civil rights. Civil rights spring from the Seventeenth and Eighteenth Centuries' reformist theories of human rights, the same ideals that inspired the English, American and French revolutions. They guarantee all citizens equal protection under the law regardless of race, religion, gender, age or disability; equal exercise of the privileges of citizenship; and equal participation in community life. Newborn babies are equal in the sense that they are entitled to as much respect for their rights as are adults.

Moral rights became enforceable civil rights for minorities and women only through great effort and vigilance. Even more effort and vigilance is required to enforce important civil rights for minors, especially for newborn babies. For the first time in history, we are poised to specify rights for minors in positive terms. Of course, these civil rights are based on their developmental needs and capacities rather than their wishes.

Adult civil rights that apply to minors include freedom from racial and gender discrimination; the right to life and personal security; freedom from slavery and involuntary servitude; and freedom from cruel, inhuman or degrading treatment and punishment. In 2005 the U.S. Supreme Court recognized the relative incapacity of minors and ruled that the execution of minors violates the cruel and unusual punishment clause of the Eighth Amendment.

The gradual emergence of minors' civil rights in the United States began through different treatment in criminal matters. The first juvenile court was established in 1899 in Cook County, Illinois. Because existing courts were not adequately rehabilitating juveniles, the U.S. Supreme Court ruling in 1967 in *In re Gault* mandated due process to provide Constitutional protections for them. Unfortunately, this did not actually improve the courts' abilities to help juveniles as much as intended.

Minors' civil rights progressed from child labor, child neglect and abuse and education laws to the idea that children have the right to environments that offer reasonable opportunities for healthy development. These include adequate nutrition, housing, recreation and health care as well as love, security, education and protection from abuse and discrimination.

These rights do not include certain adult rights such as the right to privacy, the right to confidentiality and the right to make their own choices on vital matters. All of this boils down to the right to have competent parents. Competent parenting actually is an enforceable affirmative civil right because incompetent parenting is a cause for state intervention through child abuse and neglect laws. These laws allow for the termination of parental rights by the state.

In 1968 in *Ginsberg v. New York*, the U.S. Supreme Court recognized society's interest in protecting minors from circumstances that might prevent them from becoming responsible citizens:

The state also has an independent interest in the wellbeing
of its youth…to protect the welfare of children…safeguarded
from abuses which might prevent their growth into free and
independent well-developed…citizens.

Stated positively, minors have a civil right to nurturance, to protection
and to make certain choices through age-grading statutes. Still, the fact
that parental rights are based on the right of minors to have competent
parents is not yet fully appreciated by courts or the public.

The civil right of minors to competent parents is more important than
adult rights to freedom of actions because of the adverse consequences incompetent parents impose on our society. Adult rights benefit individuals and are the backbone of our democratic society, but minors' rights are
essential for our society's survival and prosperity. Our society's wellbeing
depends on protecting and nurturing our young so that they can become
responsible citizens.

THE RIGHT TO COMPETENT PARENTS

None of us have a moral right to succeed. In fact, we have a right to fail
unless our failure adversely affects other people. The failures of parents do
affect others, including their children and society, and fly in the face of
children's right to competent parents. A person's freedom to fail therefore
faces an exception when that person is a parent.

The legal right of newborn babies to competent parents stems from
the fact that incompetent parents justify state intervention and possible
termination of parental rights. Because our society is paying an ever larger
share of the cost of rearing, educating and treating neglected and abused
children, we all have a financial stake in competent parents.

Public decision making needs to acknowledge the interests of children
and that parents usually protect those interests best. But when a parent's
inability to do so is evident before childbirth, the state is obligated by existing child abuse and neglect statutes to intervene preemptively.

Our society must value newborn babies enough to protect their rights
to competent parents and to enforce its expectations of parenthood before
childbirth. Whether or not a pregnancy was planned, the decision to enter

parenthood should be based on a newborn's right to a competent parent before the child is born. Action should not be delayed until after childbirth when maternal and paternal instincts, hormones and ideologically and fantasy-based emotions impede problem solving and decision making.

THE DEVELOPMENTAL NEEDS OF BABIES

The notion that all babies require is feeding and diapering prevails in popular thought and public policies. This is reflected in the use of the term *caregiving* rather than *parenting* as the primary need of babies and toddlers. The fact that they are interacting, learning human beings seeking to form relationships with their parents from the day of birth has not taken solid root.

Babies usually are seen as objects to be adored and cared for. This view allows us to overlook the fact that a difficult birth and time in intensive care, and even circumcision, are traumatic for newborns. It makes it possible to ignore the baby while dealing with the crisis of adolescent childbirth, including establishing paternity. It makes it possible to presume that baby boys aren't affected by the pain of circumcision. It makes it possible to ignore the connection between baby-parent love and loving adult relationships in later life. It makes it possible to successfully market videos for babies that absorb their attention and ensnare them with "infotainment" before they can explore the world on their own.

The fact that their development as human beings depends on enduring parent attachments formed through parent-child interactions is not fully appreciated by the general public in part because parenthood cannot compete with less demanding and more materially rewarding activities. Actually newborn babies are interacting persons in every sense of the word. They analyze and respond to sounds. They stop feeding to listen to something. When they hear other babies cry, they usually cry with them. They might stop crying on hearing a recording of their own voice. They gaze deeply into their mothers' eyes. They closely watch their mothers. They are upset when their mothers wear expressionless masks or when their mothers are depressed. They hunger for interaction with humans who are motivated to bond with them and can fill their survival needs. Without a doubt, they are human beings…they are persons.

Attachment Bonding

Historians, archeologists and anthropologists building on the work of Charles Darwin have described the human capacity for attachment bonding, cooperation and altruism from early life. Animal research suggests that bonding between mother and baby is encoded through genes in addition to the usual memory process. The bonding process tempers self-assertive-individual-survival instincts with integrative-species-survival instincts.

While competition is a key motivator in human affairs, cooperation is even more important. The viability of interpersonal relationships and market economies depend upon our virtuous natures. Higher brain centers evolved to ensure species survival through attachment bonding between parents and children and among intimate groups. These trust-inducing advantages contributed to neurological attachment bonding systems fostered by hormones.

The attachment bonding process begins before birth. Research on lifetime health records reveals that characteristics in later life are affected by our experiences in the womb. A classic example was the retarded growth of women who were low-birth-weight newborns during the Dutch Hunger Winter of 1944-1945 and who later gave birth to smaller babies themselves even with adequate nutrition during their pregnancies.

Newborn babies seek attachment bonds. They can form close relationships, express themselves forcefully, show preferences, form memories and influence people from day one. They show their thoughts when they reach out, give an inquisitive look, frown, scream in protest, gurgle in satisfaction or gasp in excitement. They listen intently to their mothers' voices, which they readily distinguish from other voices. They engage in complex activities that integrate their senses and enable learning.

The psychologist John Bowlby's groundbreaking theory of attachment bonding borrows from cybernetics, the study of how mechanical and biological systems self-regulate to achieve goals as their external and internal environments change. Attachment theory begins with the idea that two basic goals guide young children's behavior: safety and exploration. A child who stays safe survives; a child who explores develops the intelligence and skills needed for adult life.

These needs often oppose each other, so they are regulated by a cybernetic thermostat that monitors safety. When safe, a child explores and plays. When safety is uncertain, a switch is thrown that triggers fear and withdrawal. The attachment bonding process allows children to handle these emotions by internalizing models of their caregivers. As they mature, these working models become their self-regulating thermostats. Four kinds of interactions develop the working models children and parents build of each other.

- First is the *succorant bonding system* present at birth. It extends from infancy into adolescence and seeks bonding with parents.

- Second is the *affiliative bonding system*, which emerges during early childhood and continues into adulthood to sustain friendships.

- Third is the *sexual bonding system*, which becomes prominent after puberty, continues through adult life, and fosters romantic relationships.

- Fourth is the *nurturant bonding system*, which flowers after puberty, continues throughout life and fosters bonding to a child and intimate relationships between adults.

Development of the *nurturant bonding system* builds on the *succorant* and *affiliative* systems. In turn, those systems depend on having been nurtured in the intertwining parent-child relationship. The capacities for each system are present during early life and emerge more fully at successive levels of development. Each system is based on human needs that persist throughout life.

These systems ensure that individuals survive and produce progeny. Many people lead full lives without reproducing, but the evolutionary purpose of their interpersonal bonding is reproduction, not just companionship or sexual gratification. Stable family relationships depend upon dampening the *self-assertive individual-survival* instincts expressed through the succorant and sexual bonding systems. This is achieved by the *integrative-species-survival* instincts of the affiliative and nurturant bonding systems.

Succorant Bonding System

A baby's succorant bonding system seeks essential caregiving for the baby's physical survival through such activities as feeding and cuddling. As seen in orphanages, without attachment bonding babies fail to thrive physically and even die. Templates for succorant bonding to mother and father images appear to be genetically programmed. Interactions with additional caregivers can help babies gauge the intentions of others and elicit their care, which also can be important for survival.

Mothers who give birth are deeply attached to the human beings who were in their bodies. Prenatal exposure to the mother's voice and odors primes a newborn to respond preferentially to a birth mother. Human babies recognize the sight, sounds, smell and touch of their mothers but apparently do not recognize their fathers the same way. However, there is some evidence that genetic mothers and fathers can tell their own newborns from other newborns simply by touching their baby's hands.

At first attachment bonding is unidirectional. Over time working models of the parent are built into the baby's brain just as images of the baby are encoded in the parent's brain. A baby's distress triggers caregiving instincts in the parent. A baby's drive for succorance is reinforced by receiving nurturing from the person to whom the baby attaches.

Nurturing instincts insure that mothers are devoted to their newborns. After birth, the baby is the center of a mother's life. Physical transformations in her body continue after birth. Nurturing her baby produces hormones and inscribes new pathways in her brain that lower the amount of stimulation needed to elicit maternal responses. Breastfeeding releases oxytocin with a relaxing effect. Within days a mother can pick out her own baby's clothes by smell alone.

Without DNA testing, fathers have no way of being certain about their parentage other than what they believe to be true. Still, a strongly attached father can be more important to his baby's wellbeing than a weakly attached mother.

Affiliative Bonding System

The affiliative bonding system favors the cooperative behavior essential for the survival of the species. Also referred to as reciprocal bonding, affiliative bonding builds on one-way succorant bonding in babies and nurturant bonding in their parents. It goes beyond a child's instinctive quest for security and a parent's instincts to nurture and protect. It involves a range of two-way dimensions that include intimacy, shared humor and positive emotions.

A child succorantly attaches *to* a caregiver and affiliatively bonds through shared interactions *with* a caregiver. A parent nurturantly bonds *with* a child by responding to the child's succorant attachment. A child's initial succorant attachment grows into affiliative bonding. However, babies do not become succorantly or affiliatively bonded with genetic mothers and fathers who don't interact intimately with them.

Babies and children form succorant and affiliative bonds with adoptive parents who nurture them. Children who discover they have been adopted have socially conditioned reactions, but they do not automatically shift their bonding relationships from the adoptive parents to the genetic ones. Life experience rather than genes creates succorant and affiliative parent-child bonding.

A deep emotional bond with blood relatives also is not based on genes. It comes from reciprocal affiliative bonding that takes place through child-parent and sibling relationships. Affiliative attachment bonds are imprinted in the brain. Adoptive parents are the real parents through their succorant attachment and affiliative bonds with their children.

Affiliatively bonded adults and children build evolving images in each other's brains. They sense and respond to each other's needs. Reciprocal interactions with caregivers develop a child's capacity for higher mental functions, empathy, compassion and resilience…in essence, they develop the child's mind.

Sexual Bonding System

The sexual bonding system appears early in life in the form of the Electra and Oedipal complexes. These complexes motivate attachment bonding with the parent of the opposite sex and rivalry with the parent of the same sex. Sexual feelings and fantasies later evolve during adolescence with the eventual goal of mating and reproduction.

Lustful craving is the basic motivation for sexual union. Lust doesn't automatically result in romantic passion or the urge to attach to a mating partner. Lust's capriciousness might be part of nature's plan. It enabled our ancestors to follow two complementary reproductive strategies. If a male had one mate and two children by a female from a different band, he would double his descendents. Likewise, a female who had a mate and became involved with another might bear the latter's baby and acquire extra food and protection for her children.

Romantic passion, the elation and obsession associated with being in love, focuses courtship on one individual at a time. The process focuses the evolutionary precious time and energy spent on mating and reproduction.

Passionate love's symptoms overlap with those of heroin (euphoric wellbeing) and cocaine (energetic euphoria). When passion is spurned or thwarted, the brain reacts with negative feelings like despair, depression and rage, all of which are similar to withdrawal symptoms from heroin or cocaine usage. Most commonly the need for passionate love eventually diminishes as affiliative bonding strengthens attachment bonding between a couple.

Nurturant Bonding System

The nurturant bonding system first appears in young children's caregiving impulses. When fully expressed in parenthood and adult companionship, it fulfills the reproductive cycle.

Romantic passion doesn't necessarily turn into nurturant attachment. They are separate processes and follow different patterns. Under the influence of oxytocin, nurturing attachment grows slowly over time as lovers rely upon, care for and deepen the trust between them. Passionate love is like fire. Nurturant love is like a growing vine that intertwines two people. Parent-child and enduring intimate adult relationships are both examples of this kind of love. Nurturant attachment between them motivates partners to stay together long enough to rear their young. When disrupted, it can cause pain. The desire for nurturant attachment generally is stronger in females than in males.

Homo sapiens is a social species full of emotions finely tuned for loving, helping, sharing and intertwining our lives. There are as many ways to have enduring companionship attachments as there are couples. Underlying them all is the willingness to compromise with and tolerate a partner as well as to nurture each other.

Attachment Styles

Attachment styles emerge gradually over time. A child with a particular temperament makes bids for nurturance. A mother with a particular temperament responds or does not respond based on her mood; how overworked she is; or which childrearing expert she has been reading. Children with sunny dispositions and upbeat mothers are likely to develop secure attachment bonds. Still a dedicated mother can overcome her own and/or her child's less pleasant disposition and foster secure attachment bonding.

A parent's capacity to respond to the emotional and mental states of a newborn baby is the foundation of secure attachment bonding. These mutual experiences develop a baby's reflective capacity and create an internal sense of cohesion and interpersonal connection. Over time, babies and young children build what John Bowlby called internal working models of themselves, their parents and their relationships with others. This self-organizing internal model of a mother provides a sense of security when the mother isn't present.

Children of parents who are empathic, set firm limits and emphasize the rights and welfare of others show high levels of pro-social and compassionate behaviors. Genetic differences also play a role. In contrast in dysfunctional families, children can become frightened or angry. They can lash out or turn away from others. In steeling themselves against their own emotional pain, they become inured to the pain of others.

THE DEVELOPING MIND

We don't ordinarily think of ourselves this way, but each one of us is a complicated self-organizing system with self-organizing subsystems including the central nervous system...the seat of the mind. The development of a child's brain depends upon communication between the minds of parent and child. It occurs through observation and interaction with more knowledgeable members of the culture throughout childhood. These connections involve an energetic resonance in which information flows freely. This learning process can be exhilarating for both child and adult.

Stable mental images are formed in babies' brains as they interact with their caregivers. A baby and mother recognize each other's faces and smile, giving the baby a secure feeling. Babies form images of their parents' bodies, personalities and behavior as their minds are shaped by their parents.

A child learns to regulate emotional states in response to parental constraints. The orbitofrontal cortex in the brain operates like a clutch that disengages the sympathetic nervous system (the accelerator) and activates the parasympathetic system (the brakes). This part of the brain is especially sensitive to face-to-face communication. This is why eye-to-eye contact between parent and child helps set effective limits. The meaning of the word "no" is conveyed more clearly with eye contact than by shouting across a room. This is the basis for the parenting limit-setting maxim: "Use your feet instead of your mouth."

Learning that wishes are not automatically gratified and that one's mind and a parent's mind are separate helps a child learn self-control as well as modulate emotions and behavior in pro-social ways. The clash of separate minds and wills is essential to mental and social development.

Self-generated play enriches personal growth and the capacity for enjoyment and creativity later. The world of symbolic meaning creates awareness that one has a subjective experience…a mind of one's own. Creative imagination-stimulating pretending crystallizes a child's ideas so that the ideas become thoughts that can be thought about. When children grasp the fact that minds are independent, they acquire their own minds. They expand their own creative imaginations.

Then the insight dawns that the child is one among others. From this time on, a child can think about other people as individuals who have their own experiences. At this point, children enter society and culture. Young children who passively view television may well be less imaginative and empathic than those who engage in self-generated, creative play.

Special Considerations in Father Relationships

Most children enjoy affiliative and, to a lesser degree than with their mothers, succorant attachment bonding with fathers. Some receive inconsistent support while others are adversely affected by their father's behavior. Still others lose their fathers early in life. Some children have high levels of involvement with males other than their genetic fathers like grandfathers and uncles.

Fathers can provide emotional support to the mothers and participate in childcare whether they live with the mother or not. Fathers also can link children to their extended families and community resources. Fathers are more likely to engage children in physical and stimulating play while mothers tend to spend more time in verbal activities.

Us/Them Memes

The feelings associated with relationships that are not based on attachment bonding are based on the genetic capacity to form *us/them* feelings. These feelings are culturally transmitted through behavioral and feeling patterns called *memes*, which are ingrained mental images of our relationships that become a part of our brain structures.

Perceptions of genetic relatives are based more on our experiences with them through memes than on genes. The biological mechanisms of memes permit us to have perceptions of genetic ties even though there is no actual genetic connection. Our tribal forbearers relied heavily on the perception of genetic ties even when there were none. As time went on, the disadvantages of mating with close genetic relatives became evident and created the need to identify actual genetic kin and avoid mating with them.

An example of how kinship feelings can crop up is when a person learns of a genetic connection to another person and experiences a visceral feeling. This is an us/them feeling and is not the same as feelings associated with attachment bonding. Instead it is based on memes.

Us/them meme feelings can shift away from individuals as our perceptions of them change. For example, friendships shift depending on how attitudes between people evolve. Marriages endure because nurturant bonds develop between couples, not just because of romantic or affiliative feelings or us/them meme codes.

The emotions involved in genetic and adoptive kinship are based on secure attachment bonding rather than on genes or on us/them memes. As adopted children and their parents know, mutual love is based on attachment bonding to each other and has nothing to do with genes.

HONORING CHILDREN'S RIGHTS

Children have come a long way from when they were seen as miniature adults, and adolescence was not recognized as a developmental stage in life. We are evolving from a baseline of extreme prejudice and discrimination against children...especially against newborns, who still are murdered at parents' discretion in some parts of the world. When children were regarded as property, they had no rights at all. Now they have moral and civil rights. Our society has taken decisive steps toward overcoming juvenile ageism.

At the same time, the notion that babies need only feeding and diapering still prevails in popular thought and public policies. The facts that babies are interacting, learning human beings and that their development depends on enduring parental attachments are not fully appreciated.

The development of the brain depends upon communication between the minds of parent and child. Babies internalize working models of their parents; in this way, their developing minds are shaped by their parents' more mature minds and actions.

Minors' rights spring from human rights that specify the minimum standards of civilized behavior. They all hinge on the right to competent parents. Competent parenthood rests upon attachment bonds that promote self-respect, self-confidence and resiliency in both children and their parents. Although parental rights come from the Constitutional protection of the privacy of the family and individual liberty, they really are legal and physical custodial duties essential for the survival of our species and our nation. Parental rights deserve careful consideration.

Chapter Nine

The Rights of Parents

Today we may not blame parents for being largely instrumental in getting their boys and girls into trouble. But twenty or thirty years from now, we will have to point our finger against those parents who, because of neglect or ignorance, wittingly or unwittingly bring out the worst in their children.

DAVID ABRAHAMSEN, 1952
WHO ARE THE GUILTY?

The idea that individuals have rights springs from the vulnerability of every human being in the face of stronger forces. Our Declaration of Independence and Constitution are based on the idea that the purpose of government is not to protect the elite, nor to facilitate greed or self-interest nor to promote a religious group's agenda. Its purpose is to guarantee certain inalienable human rights for all people including our nation's *posterity*...our young citizens.

Most of us presume that parents have rights that give them exclusive power over their children, especially newborn babies. But the need to specify those rights only arises when things go wrong in families and in child-serving institutions. Unfortunately, the emotionally charged issue of parental rights arises quite often today. Parents compel state intervention when they neglect and abuse or dispute custody of their children. Minors give birth. Too many child-serving institutions are overburdened and unable to function effectively.

Even defining who is a parent can be complicated. With surrogate birth and artificial insemination, defining a mother and a father can be complicated. By eliminating the ambiguous term "natural parent" from its rules for establishing a legal parent-child relationship, the Uniform Parentage Act encourages courts to focus on the precise relationship a female or male has to a child. Is the relationship of each mother and father: 1) genetic, 2) birth (mother only), 3) functional, 4) stepparent, or 5) adoptive? A single child could have as many as nine different persons legally recognized as a parent by adding 6) foster, 7) step, 8) surrogate and 9) sperm or egg donor.

PARENTAL RIGHTS

Because of their obligations to their children, parents need rights or prerogatives to protect and fulfill the human rights of their children. Unfortunately, contemporary talk about human rights usually emphasizes the rights to benefits and overlooks the responsibilities that accompany those rights.

In the past, children have been treated as the personal property of their parents. Under Roman law, the *patria protestas* doctrine gave fathers life and death power over their children. To this day, the popular presumption is that children belong to their parents.

In contrast, since The Enlightenment of the Eighteenth Century, parenthood in Western cultures has been seen as a contract between parents and society by philosophers and evolving legal codes. Parents are awarded rights in exchange for discharging their responsibilities.

John Locke in the Seventeenth Century and William Blackstone in the Eighteenth Century held that parental rights and powers arise from their duty to care for their offspring. They recognized that no society can survive unless its children grow up to be responsible, productive citizens. Children also have the right to be raised without unjustified interference by the state. Taken together, these rights are called the *right of family integrity*. Both Locke and Blackstone held that, if a choice is forced upon society, it is more important to protect the rights of children than to protect the rights of adults.

Every man and every woman has a natural and Constitutional right to procreate. This principle could be reasonably applied when the onset of menarche was between sixteen and eighteen. Now that menarche appears on average at the age of twelve, we must ask if every girl and boy has a natural and Constitutional right to procreate. In the light of this question, the need for careful thought about parental rights and responsibilities is intensified.

THE CHILD-PARENT RELATIONSHIP

James Garbarino, professor of psychology at Loyola University Chicago, points out that parental rights are influenced by personal and public views of child-parent relationships. Are children:

- the private property of parents,

- members of families with no direct link to the state, or

- citizens with a primary relationship with the state?

Children as Private Property

Parental rights have become the most protected and cherished of all Constitutional rights. They are based on the natural right to beget children and the likelihood that affection leads parents to act in the best interests of their children. The Fourth Amendment's protection of the privacy of the home and the Fourteenth Amendment's due process clause are interpreted to give parents legal and physical custody of their children. The popular presumption that children are the property of their parents therefore is understandable.

In the 1995 Congress, a Parental Rights and Responsibilities Act was introduced. It would have created a Constitutional amendment specifying absolute parental rights. It didn't gather support because the legal system already respects parental rights. It also would have made protecting children from neglect and abuse more difficult.

In spite of strongly held beliefs to the contrary, the legal system no longer considers children as property. There even is a genetic basis for the legal position that parents do not own their children. The genes we give them are not our own. Our own genes were mixed when they were transmitted to us by our parents. Our genes are beyond our control. We really do not own them. They extend back through previous generations and potentially forward into future generations. We are only the temporary custodians of our own genes and of our children.

Mary Lyndon Shanley, professor of political science at Vassar College, holds that an individual's right to reproduce and a parent's wishes cannot be the primary foundation of family law. The primary focus must be on children's needs and interests. The parent-child relationship is one of stewardship. Parental authority involves responsibilities beyond the parent's own wishes.

What's more, our legal system is based on the principle that no individual is entitled to own another human being. Guardians of incompetent adults are agents, not owners, of those persons. In the same way, the childrearing rights of parents consist of 1) the guardianship right (legal custody) to make decisions on behalf of a child and 2) the right to physical custody of the child. These rights are based on a child's interests and needs rather than ownership of the child. We certainly do not own our children.

Children as Family Members

Children are generally regarded as family members with no direct link to the state. The concept of parental rights sprang from traditions and Constitutional precedents that endow genetic and adoptive parents with special rights.

Parental rights are legal prerogatives based on the moral and civil rights of children to be nurtured and protected. They are based on the assumption that parents can best decide how to raise a child without undue interference by the state. Without a voluntary or involuntary forfeiture of parental duties, the state cannot permanently remove children from their parents' custody to seek a better home for them unless there has been a legal termination of parental rights.

Children as Citizens

Two trends have added the view of a child as a citizen. The first is the growing emphasis on the right of children to grow up without neglect or abuse. The second is increased limitations on parental control seen in child neglect and abuse laws, child labor laws, mandatory education laws, adolescent health care policies and parental responsibility laws. When parents do not fulfill their responsibilities, child protection services intervene and governmental agencies can assume legal and physical custody. Then the child's primary relationship is with the state as custodian.

Like other guardians, parents have the legal prerogative to make stewardship decisions. Society generally defers to their authority. The challenge is to encourage parents to act in the interests of their children rather than in their own selfish interests. Toward this end, lawmakers rely on persuasion and education to help parents fulfill their obligations. Because they are unresponsive to persuasion and education, some parents require legal interventions before and after a baby is born.

THE PARENT-SOCIETY CONTRACT

James Dwyer, professor of law at William and Mary University, affirms that parental rights do not have a direct Constitutional basis. The emergence of children's rights reflects this position; our society has progressively and empirically limited the control parents have over their children's lives.

Dwyer endorses the Enlightenment view that persons who conceive and give birth enter an implicit contract with society to raise their children as responsible citizens. Damage caused by maltreatment extends beyond the individuals involved and gives our society a compelling interest in the wellbeing of our young.

Mark Vopat, professor of philosophy at Youngstown State University, also holds that a parent's obligations derive from an implicit contract with the state beyond the child. This *parent-society contract* provides a strong moral imperative for public efforts that ensure every child's safety and quality of life. Since a contract implies mutual obligations, the parents and society are accountable to each other. The government's role is reflected in debates about:

- Child wellbeing. Is it an entitlement? A privilege? A tool for social control? *The trend is to view it as an entitlement.*

- Adolescent childbirth. Who has legal and physical custody of a minor's newborn baby? *Strictly speaking no one, but relatives and government policies support minor parents by default.*

- Financial support. Is financial responsibility for a child purely a private matter or a public responsibility? *Both. Federal and state laws mandate childrearing benefits in addition to financial child support from parents and sometimes grandparents.*

In the parent-society contract, government plays a vital role in supporting parents in rearing children and preventing maltreatment. The intimacy involved in family relationships can't be provided by the state. It's the duty of families to rear children. Still, state and local governments *are* responsible for providing schools and safe neighborhoods to support childrearing. They can provide health insurance, tax deductions and welfare benefits as well.

Parents really do not need specifically defined rights. They have prerogatives that flow from their children's rights. Unfortunately, parental prerogatives and children's rights do not fit well in contemporary society. As examples, workplaces offer little accommodation for parents' childrearing duties, and, when children are held indefinitely in supposedly temporary foster care, their right to competent parents is unfulfilled.

Public policies must recognize that children have the right to be cared for by persons with an enduring commitment to, and the capacity for, parenthood. Public policies also need to recognize that in the parent-society contract, society must ensure that parents have access to essential childrearing resources. The parental rights debate would be resolved by shifting it from children as property to parenthood as a career. *Parenthood is a parent-society, contract-based career* with prerogatives derived from the responsibility to nurture a child and to advocate for the child's interests.

Being the loving mother or father of a child does not necessarily mean that one is qualified for legal and physical custodial rights. Parental love is insufficient for healthy child development. A minor or developmentally disabled person can be a loving mother or father without having parental rights. Persons even remain a mother or a father of a child after parental rights have been terminated and other parents have assumed motherhood and fatherhood roles through adoption or kinship care.

THE RIGHTS OF MOTHERS

The laws of every state give the woman or girl who conceives and bears a child automatic recognition as the legal mother. Giving birth follows the physical relationship formed during pregnancy. These laws reflect an appropriately strong bias in favor of birth mothers, especially those who care for and form attachment bonds with their babies. This is complicated by surrogates who are not genetic mothers but who have a prenatal physical relationship with a newborn.

States seldom challenge genetic/birth motherhood unless compelling circumstances arise, such as a Child in Need of Protective Services petition filed before childbirth. Even in such cases, a newborn baby may be placed in foster care under state custody with the intention of rehabilitating the genetic/birth mother. This intent usually is not realized. A similar situation exists with children whose mothers are incarcerated with the expectation of maintaining the mothers' custody of their children. A 2009 study by Volunteers of America revealed that after release of their mothers from prison 81% of their children remained with their caregivers and did not live with their mothers.

Women and girls who give birth can decline parenthood by voluntary revocation of their parental rights through a Termination of Parental Rights proceeding to allow for adoption. Paradoxically, implicit recognition that minors do not have the judgment required for parenthood is reflected in the fact that minors require a guardian *ad litem* in order to terminate their parental rights and an adult or institutional payee to receive Temporary Assistance for Needy Families benefits. An involuntary Termination of Parental Rights can be initiated after reasonable efforts to help parents meet return conditions have failed. Mothers' parental rights also can be terminated automatically at childbirth under circumstances such as previous involuntary terminations or murder of a sibling. In some states, third parties like foster parents can petition for the termination of genetic parental rights.

THE RIGHTS OF FATHERS

Unlike maternity, substantial Constitutional guidance has been provided for states in determining paternity. States must insure that men have the opportunity to seek to establish paternity. A genetic connection and a relationship with a child (or the effort to establish one) are necessary for Constitutional protection of a paternity claim.

To claim parental rights, males must register with putative father registries within varying time frames. Agencies are required to notify putative fathers of the mothers' adoption plans. Questions arise about the feasibility of making fathers aware of their need to register. In situations where genetic fathers don't want to acknowledge fatherhood, state agencies try to establish paternity through genetic testing, other biological evidence or acknowledgement by the mother or the father in order to seek child support payments.

A father's genetic tie can be overridden when a child's interests are better served by a man who is married to the mother and who has established a relationship with the child. In the 1989 U.S. Supreme Court case *Michael H. v. Gerald D.*, the genetic father of a child produced during an adulterous relationship was denied paternity in favor of the father who was actually raising the child.

PARENTAL LIABILITY

The common-law doctrine of parental immunity has maintained that, in the absence of willful and wanton misconduct, children cannot sue their parents for negligence. In response to the magnitude of child neglect and abuse, most states and courts are beginning to define parental liability. As long ago as 1963, an Illinois Appeals Court heard *Zepeda v. Zepeda* in which a child sued his father for having caused him to be born out of wedlock. Although that suit was unsuccessful, it raised the issue of a child's legal right to be wanted, loved and nurtured…in essence, to be competently parented.

Children have successfully sued their parents for negligence and have brought actions against third parties who alienate a parent from the family. In 1992 in Orlando, Florida, eleven-year-old Gregory Kingsley legally "divorced" his mother so he could be adopted by his foster parents.

THE *PARENS PATRIAE* DOCTRINE

The most significant fact justifying state involvement is that children do not choose the families into which they are born. The *parens patriae* doctrine justifies state intervention as a part of the parent-society contract. *Parens patriae* is Latin for "father of the people." The doctrine grants the inherent power and authority of the state to protect people who are legally unable to act on their own behalf. It gives state courts the ultimate power to terminate parental rights and is based on three assumptions:

- Childhood and adolescence are periods of dependency and require supervision.

- The family is of primary importance but the state should play a role in a child's education and intervene when the family fails to provide adequate nurturance, moral training or supervision.

- When parents disagree or fail to exercise their authority, the appropriate authority to determine a child's or an adolescent's interests is a public official.

The *parens patriae* doctrine empowers the state to compel parents and minors to act in ways that are beneficial to society. It never presumed that the state would assume parenting functions. Instead, the state is responsible for protecting the best interests of children under the guidance of two principles:

- The wellbeing of society depends upon children being educated and not being exploited.

- A child's developmental needs for nurturance and protection are defined by child neglect and abuse statutes.

A 1985 decision by Canada's Supreme Court made a child's welfare paramount in disputes between genetic parents and third parties. In *King v. Low*, the Court stated that although the genetic parents' claims would receive serious consideration, they must give way to the best interests of the children when the children have developed close psychological ties with another individual. This view is taking hold in American courts as well.

Our legal system distinguishes between what parents can do to themselves and what they can do to their children. For example, parents can refuse essential medical treatment themselves but usually aren't allowed to do the same with their children. They also aren't permitted to physically harm their children, nor can they allow children to physically harm themselves.

Parents who fail to provide a minimum level of care, who abandon their children or who fail to provide supervision can be found guilty of neglect. Parents who physically, emotionally or sexually abuse their children can be found guilty of abuse. Parents who have been convicted of a serious crime, who abuse drugs or alcohol or who cannot meet return conditions after their children have been removed can be found unfit as parents. When persons cannot be persuaded or educated to become competent parents within a certain period of time, parental rights can be terminated to enable adoption.

STATE LIABILITY

Despite the *parens patriae* doctrine, the liability of the state if it does not protect minors has not been clearly defined. In 1989, the U.S. Supreme Court ruled in *DeShaney v. Winnebago County Department of Social Services* that the state is not required by the Fourteenth Amendment to protect the life, liberty or property of its citizens against invasion by private actors.

> Joshua DeShaney suffered brain damage from repeated beatings by his father at the age of four. As a result Joshua was expected to remain institutionalized for life. The U.S. Supreme Court rejected arguments that the state had a duty to protect Joshua because it once placed him in foster care and later because social workers suspected he was being abused by his father but

took no action. It held that only "when the state takes a person into its custody and holds him there against his will" does the Fourteenth Amendment due process clause require officials to take responsibility for the individual's safety and wellbeing. At the same time, the Court did not rule out the possibility that the state acquired a duty to protect Joshua under tort law.

An appellate court in California upheld a local court's dismissal of a suit by a seventeen-year-old who alleged damage by mismanagement of his adoption as a newborn:

> At the age of 17, Dennis Smith filed a complaint against the Alameda County Social Services Department alleging the agency was liable for damages because it failed to find an adoptive home when his mother gave him to the Department for the purpose of adoption shortly after his birth. The Department placed Dennis in a series of foster homes, but no one adopted him.
>
> Dennis claimed that the Department negligently or intentionally failed to take reasonable actions to bring about his adoption. Therefore, he was deprived of proper and effective parental care and guidance and a secure family environment. Dennis alleged that this caused him mental and emotional damage.

The dismissal of Dennis' complaint was upheld in appellate court on a number of grounds, including the difficulty in directly linking his damage to the failure to arrange for his adoption. The court implied that liability could result with more convincing links between early life experience and later outcomes.

Cook County, Illinois, settled a claim out of court by an eighteen-year-old boy over the negligence of county social workers. In this case, the link between professional practices and damage to Billy Nichols apparently was made effectively:

> In December of 1981, attorneys for the State of Illinois and Cook County paid $150,000 in an out-of-court settlement of a suit of a former dependent child, Billy Nichols, who had been

entrusted to the child-welfare system and later as an adult sued the county social service agency for the negligence of social workers that kept Billy dependent and unfit to live in society.

On September 19, 1960, Billy and his seven-month-old sister were abandoned by their mother and found eating garbage behind a skid-row mission in Chicago. Billy's age (approximately five) was unknown, and his speech was unintelligible. He was sent to an institution for the retarded in Michigan for four years. After a subsequent stormy foster-home placement, he was placed in Cook County's juvenile security prison for nearly three years, although the superintendent repeatedly petitioned the court to remove him.

In 1969, a legal aid lawyer, Pat Murphy, filed a class-action suit to release dependent and neglected children from prison on behalf of Billy. At 14, Billy was transferred to Elgin State Hospital, where he ran away ten times and was committed to the Illinois Security Hospital at Chester at the age of 18. Three years later Attorney Murphy intervened to enroll Nichols in a psychiatric program for two years, until he was jailed for car theft.

Lawsuits continue to attempt to redress the adverse impact of foster care. Class action suits have been used to force improvements in child welfare services. In 1993 a class action suit was filed by the American Civil Liberties Union and the Children's Rights Project, Inc., against Milwaukee County and the state of Wisconsin for failing to adequately protect children. In response, the duties and authority of child welfare services were transferred from the county to a state Bureau of Milwaukee Child Welfare.

THE RIGHT TO BE A COMPETENT PARENT

To say that a parent has a right to be competent might stretch the notion of rights too far. However, the logic for this right in our society is compelling and worth considering.

First of all, by definition the child-parent unit is irreducible. One half of the unit is a parent, and one half is a child. The interests of children and the interests of parents are inseparable, and both derive from a child's goal of responsible citizenship.

When parents face dangerous environments, poverty, unemployment, illness or mental incapacities, their children inevitably face the same problems along with the risk of incompetent parenting. If children's interests are to be fulfilled, the interests of parents must also be taken into account. If children have a moral right to be competently parented, then parents have a moral right to be competent if they are not under the legal or physical custody of others.

A second reason is that the integrity of society itself depends upon competent parents. Incompetent parents threaten the stability of society and incur enormous public costs. Therefore, in this view becoming a competent parent deserves the status of a right.

Third, human beings have a genetic predisposition to parent competently in order to ensure the survival of our species. The goal of the reproductive cycle is parenthood, not just procreation. Conceiving and giving birth initiate parenthood as the fruition of the parents' own developmental stages of childhood, adolescence and adulthood. In the most fundamental sense, competent parenthood fulfills the role of a woman or a man in the reproductive cycle. In order to preserve humanity and our society, adults have a right to fulfill their reproductive and parental potentials and for the state to help them become competent parents when possible.

BALANCING THE RIGHTS OF PARENTS AND MINORS

The essence of childhood at the beginning of the Twentieth Century was its dependency. Competent parents respected this dependency by judiciously exercising their authority. In the second half of the Twentieth Century, parental authority declined. As a result, childrearing has become a negotiation between parent and child with state and other agencies monitoring the process.

In the past, children were assumed to have capabilities we now rarely think they have because their labor was needed to help a family survive. In our efforts to give our children enjoyable childhoods, we tend to downplay their developmental need to assume responsibilities and obligations. Much confusion about adolescence is caused by stressful conflicts between adolescents' rights and their obligations to their parents. This highlights minors' responsibility to accept parental authority and to cooperate with their parents.

In some ways, the contemporary adolescent quest for independence represents a return to the time in which childhood did not extend beyond fourteen. The difference is that in earlier centuries persons were economically productive at the age of fourteen and were not capable of reproduction whereas now they have an increasing number of years, often beyond adulthood, before they become economically productive.

The shift in power from adults to children and adolescents has emotional and economic repercussions. Parents may now look to their offspring for emotional support and give them excessive material goods that stress family finances. This shift includes the ability of children and adolescents to bring legal proceedings against their parents for alleged abuse without justification. All of this has eroded parental authority. This trend toward overindulgence is further abetted by the exploitation of adolescents as consumers.

Although our tradition of individual autonomy has largely kept government out of the family, the law is moving toward defining the limits of parental power. The Juvenile Justice and Delinquency Prevention Act of 1974 removed "status offenses" of incorrigibility and running away from juvenile delinquency. They are now regarded as related to inadequate or inappropriate parental authority rather than as acts stemming solely from the adolescents. The focus has shifted to therapeutic interventions.

When family matters are brought into the legal system, the interests of children, parents and the state need to be carefully identified and balanced to determine the appropriate rule of law.

VALUING THE PARENTAL RIGHTS OF COMPETENT PARENTS

If all parents and child-serving institutions served children's developmental interests, the issue of parental rights seldom would be raised.

Parental rights are no longer based on the juvenile ageist presumption that children are property. Legal and physical custodial rights enable parents to discharge their responsibilities in a parent-society contract (parenthood) that provides a strong moral imperative for public efforts to ensure children's safety and quality of life. Parental rights really are prerogatives essential for discharging the duties of parenthood.

A shift from the rights of parents to the best interests of children has gradually emerged in our courts. Parents who fail to meet specified conditions can have their parental rights terminated to permit adoption of a child. Most states have set aside the parental immunity doctrine so that children can sue their parents under certain circumstances.

We can balance the interests of children, parents and the state if we truly value competent parents.

Chapter Ten

Competent Parents: The Source of
Our Society's Strengths

*The education of a child begins not in our classrooms but in
our homes and communities. It's family first that instills the
love of learning in a child.*

PRESIDENT BARACK OBAMA
STATE OF THE UNION ADDRESS, 2010

*The only way women can achieve equal citizenship is for
the entire society to contribute to the provision of public good
that everyone desires: well-raised children who will mature
into productive, law-abiding citizens. And that means that
all free riders—from employers to governments to husbands
to communities—have to pitch in and help make the most
important job in the world a top national priority and a
very good job.*

ANN CRITTENDEN
THE PRICE OF MOTHERHOOD

An eight-year-old outwits burglars in the movie *Home Alone*. A ten-year-old can explain the intricacies of a computer to an adult. A twelve-year-old can get a babysitter license from the Red Cross. Why can't a sixteen-year-old enter parenthood?

In the popular view, especially among people who have never been parents, parenthood is as simple as babysitting. Parenthood is seldom clearly recognized as a developmental stage of adulthood that follows adolescence and that complements childhood.

Parenthood meets the needs of parents as well as children. It satisfies their biological drive to procreate and nurture. It fulfills the parents' and the children's needs for intimate relationships. These rewards of parenthood are more readily appreciated by parents who had good relationships with their own parents than by those who did not.

Parenthood is hard work. Like any career, it expands your perspective, knowledge and skills. Unlike other careers, it is a financial cost rather than a source of income. The U.S. Department of Agriculture estimates that it costs over $286,000 to raise one child for seventeen years.

Parenthood is responsibility for the life—the legal and physical custodianship—of another person. A newborn baby is a person. An individual can have no greater responsibility in life. The essential prerequisite for assuming responsibility for another person's life is the ability to be responsible for your own life. Readiness for parenthood follows adolescence.

VALUING COMPETENT PARENTS

Thirty years ago we were assured that technology would give us more leisure time for our families. The opposite has occurred. The disappearance of the family wage, based on the principle of one breadwinner in a family, has necessitated more than one income. The more we can do, the more we want to do. The more money we have, the more money we want. Yet most of us yearn for deeper fulfillment.

One way to find fulfillment is to share the wonders of life by growing with our children. Too many parents and other adults miss this opportunity by doing things for, rather than with, children. Too many parents have little time for their children. Even worse, too many families are dysfunctional.

Why does our society adulate children but fail to recognize parenthood as essential to our nation's prosperity? One reason is that emulating the audacious behavior of celebrities and acquiring wealth often eclipses family relationships. Having children can be more important than raising them. Acting like adolescents can be more important than parenting them. All of this fosters unstable relationships that result in divorce, cohabitation and adolescent childbirth. All of this denigrates parenthood.

Most importantly, the fact that childrearing families subsidize our society isn't fully appreciated. Governments and businesses really are free riders that depend on the labor of parents so that our youth will become productive citizens. Our society owes parenthood a social and financial debt, which is recognized to a degree through tax benefits. Even those of us without children gain when parents raise children who become productive workers who contribute to our economy and to our national security.

We need a vision for America in which the economic benefits of parenthood are valued as much as those of paid careers.

WHY WE NEED TO VALUE COMPETENT PARENTS

As we move on into the Twenty-First Century, we clearly understand the pleasures we seek from material things. But we are only beginning to envision the kind of citizens our nation needs.

The vitality of our science, technology and economy enabled the United States to lead the world at the end of the Twentieth Century. We benefited from a high standard of living and unprecedented freedoms. But our advantages have eroded as knowledge has become widespread and low-cost labor has become readily available globally. The National Academy of Sciences, our most prestigious scientific voice, calls for a comprehensive federal effort to bolster our competitiveness so we will gain rather than lose from globalization.

Without a major push to strengthen America's competitiveness, we will lose our advantages. Economic progress comes from new industries created by the ideas of exceptional scientists and engineers. Continuing to improve our human capital as we move into a knowledge era depends upon a well-educated, productive citizenry.

Our society's wellbeing has traditionally been measured by the goods and services produced and consumed as measured by the GDP. As was made clear in Chapter One, the GDP alone does not measure the wellbeing of our society. People suffering long, expensive illnesses have more economic value than when they are healthy. Expenditures for social services and prisons also increase the GDP.

The National Academy of Sciences points out that working more to spend more on goods and services disconnects us from our communities and our society. Alexis De Tocqueville, the Nineteenth Century French observer of America, predicted this outcome when he highlighted individualism in the United States:

> The prospect really does frighten me that they will become so engrossed in the cowardly love of immediate pleasures that their interest in their own futures and in that of their descendants may vanish, and that they will prefer to tamely follow the course of their destiny rather than make a sudden energetic effort necessary to set things right.

Richard Florida, professor of public policy at George Mason University, calls attention to the obvious fact that the key to the global economy no longer is competition for goods, services or capital. It is competition for creative people…for human capital. Creativity is a common good like liberty and security. If left unnourished, it will slip away.

Unlike other developed nations, our society doesn't place a high value on competent parents. We have the highest child poverty rates and the lowest childrearing benefits. We also have the highest incarceration rates. We no longer can afford to focus only on economic factors that contribute to our social problems. Inadequate, strained and disrupted parent-child relationships are far more important. At the core of society's lonely, unhappy undercurrent lies an inability to form and sustain intimate relationships resulting from self-centered individualism with a consequent lack of concern for others and an inability to collaborate in teamwork.

Besides its economic effects, the prevalence of divorce has shaped attitudes toward the formation of families. Even in families that don't split up, children can grow up fearful that it could happen at any time. Some young people have responded by avoiding long-term commitments. This mirrors the transient nature of jobs, living situations and other aspects of their lives.

Secure attachment bonding with competent parents during the early years fosters a child's ability to commit to others. Competent parents prevent our social problems. Incompetent parents create and/or contribute to them. We must confront the belief that little can be done to strengthen families and that institutions must assume the responsibility of childrearing. Since childcare, schools and professionals try to fill in when parents fail, parents aren't held as responsible for their actions with their own children as they are for their actions with people outside their families. The counterproductive trend is to blame schools rather than parents when children fail in school.

On the positive side, many women and men choose to give their careers as parents as high or higher priority as paid work. Many struggling parents receive and benefit from education and support. Family-friendly neighborhoods and communities are being created. Parents have increasing access to private and public resources. These trends reflect our cultural expectation that all children should grow up to be responsible citizens.

OUR CULTURAL EXPECTATION OF COMPETENCE

Because adult interests overshadow children's interests, our society has not clearly spelled out its cultural expectations of parents. The general assumption is that parents will raise their children as they wish, although it is expected that young people will be educated. The lack of articulated cultural values doesn't mean that they don't exist.

The United States is a value-based nation founded on the cultural presumption that all human beings are created equal and endowed with certain rights to an opportunity to competent personal fulfillment. Our values inspired the Declaration of Independence, the Constitution and the Bill of Rights. They evolved from ideas about freedom and justice that accommodate diverse ethnicities and beliefs. They are generally shared by our various ethnic subcultures. The Supreme Court has affirmed that children are persons who have rights under the Constitution. A newborn baby clearly does have a Constitutional right to have an opportunity to become a competent adult.

Competence in Business and Government

Our cultural expectation of competence is embedded in regulations that curb the exploitation of individuals by others and the marketplace. We expect that telephones will work, that checks will be honored, that prices will be honestly displayed, that the contents of foods will be labeled, that contracts will be honored, that manufactured goods will be warranted, that schedules will be dependable, that laws and regulations will be enforced and that service providers will be licensed. Travel in many foreign countries makes us realize how much we take these cultural expectations for granted.

We expect competence and responsibility in business and professional transactions in the United States because of our laws and regulations based on our cultural values. Compliance with these expectations depends upon people holding values that support competence and responsibility. Persons who have not internalized these values exploit others on grand scales as white-collar criminal and on smaller scales as blue-collar criminals.

Competence in Parenthood

The stark exception is that our society does not explicitly expect the genetic parents of children to be competent, even as we explicitly require competence for individuals who would adopt children. Because our society holds no specific expectations for parents who conceive and give birth, child neglect and abuse have reached epidemic proportions. Our rates exceed that of all other developed nations. We only intervene after child neglect and abuse have occurred, and often then the efforts are ineffective.

Enormous public expenditures for treatment, rehabilitation and incarceration result. At a rate of over 900,000 cases investigated and substantiated annually over the last seventeen years, over 11 million of our children have been neglected or abused. Many will become habitual criminals or welfare dependent. All of this would change dramatically if our vision was that all our children will be raised by competent parents.

Children become responsible adults when they internalize the values of competent parents. Parents set limits the children learn to respect. Children become responsible for their behavior when their parents acknowledge their own mistakes as well.

Still, cultural expectations of parental competence are relatively recent in human history. This may partially explain why these expectations are not obvious to everyone. American cultural values support raising children to become responsible citizens capable of committed attachments and of contributing to the common good. The cultural expectation of parents is that they will develop both children's and parents' potentials as responsible citizens. Family relationships are as important for adults as they are for children. The family is still the only institution that provides unconditional acceptance for both. Childhood and parenthood are vital life stages for developing competence and personal responsibility.

Fortunately, our pluralistic American cultural values are a rich source of principles. All but a few antisocial subcultures agree that children need dependable, nurturing environments and competent adults with whom they can form enduring attachment bonds. They agree that the family is the primary agent for child development, especially as it relates to character and self-discipline. They agree that the objective of childrearing is to develop an individual's ability to function competently and responsibly within society.

Our cultural values define clear boundaries between childhood and parenthood. When those boundaries are blurred, the rights of children and parents are not balanced by their responsibilities. These rights surface when divorce or child abuse or neglect occur, but they also occur in daily family life as the question of whose way will prevail arises. Competent parents ensure that their wills prevail.

THE EVOLUTION OF CULTURAL PARENTAL VALUES

Families originated from clans where fathers had absolute power over their wives and children. In medieval times, parents coped with excess heirs or unwanted children by selling them, giving them to the church as oblates or abandoning them.

The Jewish tradition introduced marriage as a sacred bond between a husband and a wife with procreation as its goal. Fathers remained the heads of households but no longer wielded absolute power over children. Christianity introduced the idea that wives and husbands should respect each other and that children were autonomous beings whose primary loyalties were to God. Still, in the Eighteenth Century, many European mothers abandoned babies or sent them to wet-nurses. Some desperately poor mothers committed infanticide.

The Industrial Revolution stripped away many of the family's functions, removing its importance as the dominant economic institution of the

Agricultural Age. Production moved out of homes, and education shifted to schools. More recently, the trend in developed countries has been to side-step the nuclear family as the preferred unit for childbearing and childrear-ing. The results are fatherless families, uncommitted parents and unprece-dented levels of child neglect and abuse that necessitate more governmental involvement and add to the burdens of public schools.

The economic and social conditions that foster marriage have not been maintained. Non-marital childbearing is both a consequence and a cause of poverty. *At the same time, when marriage and motherhood are idealized and employed women are devalued, non-nuclear families can be viewed inappropriately as deviant and unworthy. This attitude undermines realistic and humane family policies.*

As a result, an incomplete understanding of the responsibilities of par-ents is common today. As one father explained, those responsibilities can strain marriages and lead to divorce:

> When a child was added to my life, it was as if something enor-mous and coveted was subtracted in return, and the transac-tion left me reeling, like someone who'd just gambled away his soul...We became slaves to this tiny new thing living in our home, and there was no going back...My wife seemed to consider me selfish and irresponsible. She was tired, she'd say, of parenting both of us...Eventually, my wife and I divorced, but our split actually enhanced my relationship with my kids. (We had twin girls after my son.) It forced me to locate my in-ner parent....

Relying on science and technology instead of on our culture for par-enting guidance also contributes to ambiguity over parenting styles. The blurred boundaries are caused in part because parents don't clearly define children's responsibilities. When parents aren't in charge, children's natural exploitative tendencies can make parenthood especially stressful and de-prive children of learning self-discipline...the foundation of moral values. In these situations, delegating parenting to childcare workers and teachers can be appealing to parents.

Research even is being conducted on whether mothers and fathers mat-ter to children. In her book *The Revolution in Parenthood: The Emerging Global*

Clash between Adult Rights and Children's Needs, Elizabeth Marquardt asks: Are children commodities to be produced by the marketplace? What role should the state have in defining parenthood? When adult rights clash with children's needs, how should the conflict be resolved? She says our society will either answer these questions through serious reflection and public debate or they will be answered for us by the marketplace. The choice is ours. At stake is the integrity of the foundation of our society: parenthood that ensures the wellbeing of our children. Unfortunately, our cultural values are not enforced until after children have been neglected or abused. Even then, conflicting social values often trump cultural values.

Our culture values competence. Valuing competent parents requires a paradigm shift from self-assertive social values to integrative cultural values.

THE TENSION BETWEEN SOCIAL AND CULTURAL VALUES

Our culture values parenthood; our society does not. Our cultural values stem from past experience and are expressed through traditions that affirm our hopes and aspirations for the future. They bind us together and help us solve human problems. They are encoded in our laws. Our social values identify what we consider important, such as material comfort, wealth, competition, and individualism. Social values are reflected by the people who receive the most adulation, such as professional athletes and celebrities.

When social and cultural values conflict, our society's integrity depends upon the cultural value prevailing in the long run through transmission from one generation to the next. The philosopher John Rawls said, "I assume that the sense of justice is acquired gradually by the younger members of society as they grow up. The succession of generations and the necessity to teach moral attitudes (however simple) to children is one of the conditions of human life."

The philosopher Michael McFall adds that child maltreatment often eliminates the trust needed for social cooperation. It also increases the chances that children will become envious of others and threaten social stability as teenagers.

History demonstrates that self-assertive social values dominate until their excesses provoke a counter-reaction based on cultural integrative values. Our social values have become detached from our cultural values in critical ways. The most obvious example is in our underclass. Historian Carl Nightingale spent six years with young black people in a Philadelphia ghetto and saw how they were saturated with our society's self-assertive social values.

> From designer sportswear to gold jewelry, they turned to expensive material goods to bolster self-respect and resorted to violence to obtain money to buy them. To compensate for the humiliation and frustration of poverty and racism, they turned to our society's self-assertive consumerism.

Nightingale found that these young people were detached from our integrative cultural values of personal and collective responsibility because they had never been exposed to these values.

Political issues often revolve around conflicts between social values associated with individual liberty and cultural values that affirm the common good. Nowhere is this more evident than in attitudes toward parenthood.

Self-Assertive Social Values	Integrative Cultural Values
Parental rights	Parental responsibilities
Passion (follow emotions)	Wisdom (thoughtful reasoning)
Gratification now	Postponing gratification
Avoiding discomfort	Tolerating frustration
Freedom to make decisions	Capacity to make decisions
Reproductive liberty	Capacity to enter parenthood
Baby as a parent's property	Baby's right to a competent parent

In the United States, self-assertive social values dominate integrative cultural values and devalue parenthood. As shown in Chapter Three the support of adolescent parents is one major sign of the way in which the social values of following one's emotions, gratification now, avoiding discomfort, the freedom to make decisions and reproductive liberty lead to viewing a baby as an adolescent mother's property. We need to align our self-assertive social values with our integrative cultural values.

ALIGNING OUR SOCIAL AND CULTURAL VALUES

People in our society have a palpable yearning for both fulfilling careers and fulfilling family lives. Aligning the social and cultural values that affect families would relieve the conflict. To achieve this alignment, we need to identify an issue; discuss it in organizations and the media; and persuade through editorials, essays and political activities. Legislation ultimately crystallizes our cultural values in laws.

Racism, for example, was expressed though slavery. A cultural value contradicted slavery but that value did not penetrate all of American society. Through a long process, slavery was identified as racism, the issue was discussed, people learned about its harmful effects and ultimately the Civil War led to the Thirteenth Amendment to outlaw slavery. In the following decades, self-assertive social values ultimately aligned with integrative cultural values through a series of laws that prohibit racial discrimination.

More recently, the cultural value of protecting children from harm was identified, discussed, educationally disseminated and ultimately crystallized as a social value in state laws that protect children from neglect, abuse, exploitative labor and accidents (by requiring the use of child car seats, for example). Mandatory education and immunization laws also protect the developmental interests of children.

Still articulating and implementing our cultural values requires thoughtful debate and problem-solving actions that are in short supply in our contemporary society. In his book *The Middle Mind: Why Americans Don't Think for Themselves*, Curtis White points out that until recently the world has experienced rapid but turbulent technology-driven growth. Efficient production and commerce have converted human and natural resources into products and services. These organizational designs function well during periods of stability with limitless resources but they break down in highly interdependent environments with limited resources. Unfortunately, when faced with the need for widespread institutional change, we prefer to wait until external forces force us to change.

Cognitive psychologists point out that we have different brain systems for handling risks. Our forebrain works analytically by considering costs and benefits. Our reptilian brain works from feelings by reacting impulsively to the unknown. The prospect of change makes us feel anxious due to the dangers of the unknown. Consequently, while making decisions, our brains grapple with multiple impulses and emotions. They can be our best guides, or they can lead us blindly astray.

What's more we have a "finite pool of worry." We are unable to maintain one fear when a different fear—a plunging stock market, a personal emergency—comes along. We simply move one fear into our worry bin and shove a different fear out. Even if we could remain concerned about an issue, we have a crisis-recoil bias, a tendency to do the easiest thing even if it doesn't resolve the issue and leaves us where we started.

When the solution to a problem lies in changing individual behavior, a person asks, *What's in it for me?* Ordering the choices can be helpful. Considering long-term benefits can lead to a different decision than if only short-term costs are considered. Although persuasion and education gain compliance from most people, a segment of the population doesn't respond. Because an individual's freedom to act then must be constrained so that others are not harmed, legislation ultimately is necessary.

Laws are an essential part of the sequence *persuasion, education and regulation* that is necessary in any public effort to change private behavior. Even private swimming pools need to be governed by state and local laws to prevent accidents and ensure safety. Our cultural values are expressed through legislation and laws some of which are designed to support families.

COMPETENT PARENTS NEED FAMILY RESOURCE SYSTEMS

As it now stands, the link between incompetent parents and social problems is obscured by other issues. Little public attention is devoted to the facts that parents can be held accountable to society through child labor, mandatory education and child neglect and abuse laws. There is even less awareness that parenthood is a privilege that merits public monitoring and support because it is vital to the future of our nation.

The responsibilities of motherhood are better known than the responsibilities of fatherhood. As long as boys fail to postpone fatherhood until they are employed and men do not support their children, mothers and children will remain trapped in poor neighborhoods. Increasing the number of fathers involved in childcare means improved employment opportunities and workplace policies that include paternity leaves, flexible scheduling, employment-based childcare and reasonable workloads. It means access to parent counseling to help couples manage disagreements and keep fathers involved. It means mentoring and community programs that model responsible fatherhood.

All of us depend upon the quantity and quality of other peoples' children. Our cultural values expect that even adults who are not parents must support the next generation. Support in return for service is an American rationale that combines individual freedom and the common good. Social Security and the post-World War II GI Bill are prime examples.

In the 1970s most developed nations began to publicly support parents. They refused to accept, as we do, the risks posed by the inadequate care of babies and toddlers. These governments now protect children through paid parental leave for childbirth and sick child care, regulated and subsidized childcare services and flexible work hours. President Nixon vetoed the Comprehensive Child Development Act in 1971. Passed with bipartisan Congressional support, this Act would have provided parents similar support in the United States.

One consequence of that veto is that all states fell far short of meeting basic childcare requirements in 2005 according to the National Association of Child Care Resource & Referral Agencies. Out of 150 possible points, the average state score was 70. Although Americans work much longer and more irregular hours than Europeans, we provide far less childcare and family leave. We would profit from adopting the support other developed countries offer parenthood.

In order to thrive, competent parents require family resource systems that include quality health care and education; a vital economy and low rates of unemployment; thriving urban centers and rural communities; safe neighborhoods; and a sense of common purpose underwritten by personal responsibility and accountability. As it now stands, families in the United States have access to some degree to family support systems that vary in the proportion of private and government funding. Our goal should be that these family support systems are able to meet the needs of all of our families.

Family Resource System		
PARENTAL RESPONSIBILITIES	PRIVATE RESOURCES	PUBLIC RESOURCES
INCOME	Self-employed Employment	Dependent tax deductions Welfare-to-work payments
HEALTH	Self-payment Insurance or HMO	Medical assistance Social security insurance
EDUCATION	Private schools Home schooling	Public schools School vouchers
CAREGIVING	Relative childcare Home childcare Center childcare Workplace childcare	Subsidized childcare Tax deductions Welfare-to-work subsidies
FAMILY STABILITY	Grandparents Private family services Friends and relatives	Family resource networks Child protective services Temporary out-of-home care

THE UNITED STATES IS NOT A FAMILY-FRIENDLY NATION

Unfortunately, parenthood is not sufficiently recognized as a career in the United States that deserves public encouragement and support. Family-friendly social policies would go a long way toward removing the need to choose between unpaid parenthood and a paid career. If women were assured of childcare and economic assistance while pursuing higher education and career development during their childbearing years, fewer would delay childbearing until later ages with all of its attendant risks and problems. For example, simple adjustments in college professors' tenure track policies would accommodate the childrearing responsibilities of mothers and fathers.

Although individual parents have little power, local, state and national organizations could recognize the service parents provide through their personal sacrifices and the resources they require for effectively pursuing the life-long career of parenthood.

Chapter Eleven

The Parenthood Career

The institution of the family is decisive in determining not only if a person has the capacity to love another individual but in the larger sense whether he is capable of loving his fellow men collectively. The whole of society rests on this foundation for stability, understanding and social peace.

MARTIN LUTHER KING, JR., 1965

Parenthood involves more than childrearing. It is the legal and physical custody of a child as child and parent grow together. Most parents successfully raise their children without consciously experiencing parenthood's developmental phases. They enhance their coping skills, altruism and self-respect as they work through their own unresolved developmental issues. For example, being a parent activates both positive and negative memories of relationships with one's own parents.

People who successfully master these challenges achieve new levels of psychological and emotional maturity along with their children. Carolyn

Newberger, professor of psychology at Harvard University, described how parenthood moves from egoistic to integrative phases:

Phase 1: Egoistic
>   Parents are self-focused and see their children as exten-
>   sions of themselves.

Phase 2: Conventional
>   Perspectives shift from self-centeredness to childrear-
>   ing practices drawn from traditions, experts and age-
>   related norms.

Phase 3: Individualistic
>   Children are viewed as unique individuals.

Phase 4: Integrative
>   Parents learn and mature with their children in their
>   families, communities and society.

Most parents intuitively meet their challenges. Many need help learning how to grow with their children. Some need education and clinical treatment to function competently. A comparatively small percentage but critically large number is unable to function competently. Typically these are adolescents and dependent adults.

We Need a Paradigm Shift

The family is the most fragile of all human institutions, yet it is the bedrock of civilization. Its strength lies in the cohesion and loyalty of the parent-child relationship from which the larger world of kin, community and nation evolves. Our moral stature and our social organization flow from parenthood. It is the source of the work ethic as well as our human capital. Self-assertive social and integrative cultural values are blended in the crucible of parenthood.

Families produce future generations. They protect members against ill health, old age, unemployment and other hazards. Especially in the United States, family relationships are strained by the tension between self-assertive social values and integrative cultural values. Is a child a parent's private property? Or is a parent a child's temporary legal and physical custodian?

Both the extreme political left and the right espouse self-assertive values that regard children as private property. The far left stresses the freedom of parents to do as they wish. The far right stresses the privacy of the family. Both extremes assert that parenthood is outside the public domain. Both avoid holding parents responsible for their children's behavior. To do so is "parent blaming," they say.

These extreme self-assertive views need to be balanced by integrative values. But the act of balancing them creates friction between competing personal interests as well as between "the world as it is" and "the world as it ought to be." Like the encircling polarities of the Chinese yin/yang symbol, *the world that is* and *the world that ought to be* are intertwined.

THE WORLD THAT IS

Self-assertive capitalism regards the family as a unit for generating money that will be spent on goods and services. It creates winners and losers and undermines reciprocity, altruism and mutual obligation...vital ingredients for the common good. Ironically, self-assertive capitalism weakens the civil society without which the marketplace itself cannot survive.

All wealthy nations, including the United States, are welfare states... that is, they are primarily capitalist states with large, selective doses of socialism. In *Wealth & Welfare States: Is America a Laggard or Leader?*, Irwin Garfinkel, Lee Rainwater and Timothy Smeeding point out that by its nature, capitalism produces too much economic insecurity. The objective of state welfare institutions is, therefore, to reduce economic insecurity.

Certain institutions—families, congregations, service clubs, athletic groups, parent-teacher associations and social organizations—offset self-assertive capitalism. They hold our society together, but they are under pressure.

Families have become money machines that generate income to pay off debts. Work schedules are more important than family schedules. Undisciplined consumption is encouraged. Television pumps out images that oppose cultural integrative values. *The desire for status is so strong that children attempt to display their worthiness through material things others want or envy. Low-income families struggle to provide these items so their children can achieve some degree of status in school. In contrast, if children are involved in extracurricular, family or community-oriented activities, they don't need to consume to achieve status.*

If we were a true materialistic society, we would value making, using and keeping material things for functional and aesthetic purposes. We would value and enjoy natural and manufactured goods. Instead we are a consumer society in which commodities are sold and discarded. Our economy depends upon planned obsolescence, a throw away orientation.

Unfortunately, promoting consumption of disposable commodities carries over into human relationships. People are viewed as means to an end. They are only consumers of goods and services. Producers and service providers have no commitment beyond satisfying the needs and pleasures of consumers.

This attitude leaks out to color all kinds of relationships. It's most obvious in the temporary "hook-up" sexual affairs seen today, but it also permeates family relationships. Cohabitation avoids the legal obligations of marriage. Marriage is seen as disposable when one partner no longer meets the other's needs. Children can be designed through technical procedures and gestated by surrogates. They can be adopted if an individual has enough money to pay others to obtain them. Children have become commodities.

In *Shattered: Modern Motherhood and the Illusion of Equality*, Rebecca Asher describes how women who set off on a footing of equality with their partners are betrayed by them when babies arrive. Mothers become "foundation parents" and de facto "household drudges," condemned to professional sidelining and part-time jobs because fathers fail to pull their weight. Mothers feel victimized, fathers feel guilty. The pair that started out on an equal-opportunity journey through life ends up sniping at each other, or scoring weary points. Many split up.

Internationally, the commodification of children is blatantly obvious. Worldwide, 1.2 million children are abducted, bought and sold each year. Every day children as young as nine are abducted or taken under false pretenses from their villages by human traffickers. These girls and boys are promised good jobs and good pay but they end up working in brothels, mines and sweatshops. For example, more than 200,000 Nepalese girls are believed to be victims of this international trade.

In the United States, the commodification of children is less obvious, but here are some examples:

- A Texas Senator proposed a bill that would permit a $500 payment to each woman who places a child for adoption rather than have an abortion. The intention was to provide an incentive to avoid abortion and make an adoption plan. Such a proposal implies that a value can be set on a newborn baby—$500 in this case. It ignores the costs of pregnancy, pre-natal care, childbirth and any complications thereof.

- Rebecca Taylor tried to sell her 5-month-old boy for $10,000. Taylor never bonded with the child and needed the money to get another apartment. She was charged with offering the sale of a child.

- Through *Fertility Choices Worldwide* the cost of hiring a surrogate mother to produce a baby can range from $103,000 to $165,000, although she receives a fraction of the cost.

CHALLENGES FOR PARENTS

Parenthood is an economic burden for too many parents. In the United States, our society expects parents to rear their children without adequate resources. The lack of childcare, health care and effective education saps the rewards of parenthood and is detrimental to our society. Parents are distracted by:

- The decline of committed, sacrificial relationships that results in weak family bonds;

- Viewing children as extensions of themselves rather than as life companions;

- Pleasing children rather than expecting them to contribute to family wellbeing;

- Guilt for being imperfect parents; and

- Stress that makes employment away from home attractive and that strains parental relationships.

Efforts to integrate childrearing and employment demonstrate the consequences of delegating parenting functions. After sixty years, the Israeli kibbutzim modified the care of babies and toddlers in separate children's houses because of its negative effects on parent-child relationships and on adult outcomes. The inability of Kibbutz-raised children to engage in intimate personal relationships was traced to early environments lacking cohesion and continuity because of transient, superficial interactions with caregivers. Virtually all kibbutz babies now receive maternal care at home during their first year of life as their mothers gradually return to the workplace. In the United States, it will take years to assess the long-term effects of today's delegated childcare of babies and toddlers on child development and adult outcomes.

THE WORLD THAT OUGHT TO BE

Commercial marketing uses *world as it ought to be* symbols. Slogans such as *Be all that you can be, Reach out and touch someone,* and *Own a piece of the rock* focus on appealing cultural values.

John Maynard Keynes concluded in the 1930s that unchecked "animal spirits"—emotions, human impulses, enthusiasms and misperceptions— drive the economy into booms and busts in a market system that fails to govern itself. On the other hand, tempered by government and safely channeled into healthy capitalism, these same animal spirits can be a source of entrepreneurial energy and benefit everyone.

Most modern social and environmental problems like ill health, lack of community, violence, drugs, obesity, mental illness, long working hours and large prison populations are more likely to occur in a society with large gaps between classes. Addressing inequality in our society would benefit everyone, the well-off as well as the poor.

Our young people's social, economic, health and educational problems require integrative community and social efforts that include racial and cultural diversity. Still our service systems often view children and youth separately from their families and communities. Programs for different categories of problems treat children as freestanding units and focus on school, peer, social class, racial, neighborhood and societal factors rather than on their homes.

These problems could be minimized if our society recognized that parenthood is a career with economic and social value and that it is our society's foundation. This would shift the balance from self-centered consumerism to a friendlier and more integrative society.

Because competent parents are essential for our society's survival, minimum legal standards should be set for determining a person's readiness to assume these responsibilities.

READINESS FOR PARENTHOOD

In most states, minors over sixteen can obtain a marriage license with the consent of parents or guardians. Kansas and Massachusetts specify twelve for females and fourteen for males. New Hampshire specifies thirteen for females and fourteen for males. If there is no parent or guardian, or if the guardian is an agency or department, consent can be given by a court. Marriage and military service can be regarded as acts of emancipation from minority status.

In contrast, most European nations make eighteen the minimum age for marriage. In Malta, people may marry from the age of sixteen, although paradoxically the age of consent for sexual intercourse is eighteen. In Turkey, the legal age for marriage is seventeen for girls and boys. In Ireland, a court can authorize the marriage of minors less than eighteen under certain conditions.

Decision-making that leads to adolescent parenthood can be flawed and is an appropriate concern for public policy. In reality, immaturity renders a minor incapable of truly informed consent about marriage or becoming a parent. State laws governing marriage age and emancipation need to be updated to conform with the physical and psychological realities of adolescent development.

In spite of the rhetoric against adolescent pregnancies, our society does little to prepare parents for their new responsibilities. Dependent adult and young adolescent childbirths from unplanned and planned pregnancies are generally considered inevitable. These vulnerable parents, it is assumed, will somehow learn to handle parental responsibilities after the children are born.

Most of the literature about adolescent pregnancy and parenthood doesn't distinguish between minor and legally adult adolescents. Late adolescent 18 to 21-year-olds are usually considered adults.

Giving birth to a baby doesn't produce an adult brain or eliminate adolescent developmental issues. John Mitchell, a developmental psychologist, calls attention to romanticized notions that can hide elementary facts:

> Romanticizing adolescence blinds us to the adolescent's capacity for life-diminishing choices. Romantics refuse to tally the teen suicides, runaways, juvenile sex trade, prisoners, broken mothers, damaged infants, and abusive fathers. In order to mature, the natural talent of youth must be aimed and trained.

Many adolescents are wishful thinkers who lack a future orientation because of their sense of invulnerability and their attraction to risk. They are easily swayed by the belief "it can't happen to me." This flavor underlies the attitude "I don't care about that now" despite knowing that cigarettes, drugs, noise and steroids produce diseases, addiction and hearing loss while shortening lifespans. Babies and young children must be protected from these characteristics.

Adolescents who become pregnant have difficulty envisioning alternatives and reasoning through the consequences of childbirth. I had the following conversation with a fifteen-year-old white girl from a middle-class family:

> Doctor: I'm told that the test results show that you are pregnant.
> Patient: My boyfriend and I knew it because the condom broke.
> Doctor: What do you plan to do?
> Patient: I'm going to have my baby and keep it. My boyfriend will drop out of school to support us.
> Doctor: Do you think that you are old enough to raise a child?
> Patient: No. I certainly wouldn't try to get pregnant.
> Doctor: Then how is it that you plan to raise this baby?
> Patient: Oh, it was an accident. Besides, I don't like school, and I can get money to live on. I know a lot of kids who are doing it.

Adolescents who become pregnant are unprepared for the decision-making and responsibilities involved in parenthood. Mature adolescents recognize that they are not ready for parenthood and terminate their pregnancies or make an adoption plan.

DOES THE BIOLOGICAL RIGHT TO PROCREATE EXTEND TO PERSONS OF ANY AGE?

The progress of our society has been based on the rule of law, the tangible repository of our cultural values. We are able to transact business with checks and credit cards rather than cash because of the trust we have in the enforcement of our laws. Yet we are still reluctant to legislate standards for competent parenthood. The prime example is our failure to deal with the crisis of adolescent childbirth.

In the United States, there is a strong emphasis on reproductive freedom. The U.S. Supreme Court described the right to procreate as a basic liberty in 1942 in *Skinner v. Oklahoma*. This has been interpreted as establishing the right to procreate. The political right might oppose the termination of any pregnancy and urge girls on to childbirth. The political left might hold that minor adolescents have the right to procreate when physically able to do so.

GirlMom.com describes itself as a "politically progressive, left-aligned, pro-choice, feminist" website that supports young mothers in their struggle for reproductive freedom and social support. It holds that adolescents are socially conditioned to believe they are irresponsible. This creates a self-fulfilling prophecy in which adolescent parents believe they can't parent well and therefore don't. For *GirlMom.com* adolescent parenthood is not a crisis; the crisis is that adolescent parents do not receive enough public support.

Kristin Luker, a professor of sociology at the University of California-Berkeley, points out that adolescents have raised healthy children throughout human history. She overlooks the fact that the average onset of menstruation has dropped from sixteen to twelve years of age. She holds that when good prenatal care and nutrition are available, the adolescent years are the best time to have babies from a physical point of view. Luker believes that "the jury is still out on whether or not adolescents make 'bad' parents."

Sara Ruddick, professor emeritus at New School University, hopes that the youngest mothers will have the resources to which all mothers are entitled. These viewpoints reflect a widely held belief that parenthood, as with procreation, is a right rather than a privilege.

These views conflict with the moral and legal principle that a child is not the property of the genetic parent. From the moral point of view, parenthood is not a right awarded by procreation. As adoptive parents well know, it is earned by nurturing a child. From the legal point of view, genetic parents hold legal and physical custodian rights that are defined and can be revoked under child neglect and abuse laws. People who require legal and physical custodians themselves cannot be the legal and physical custodians of other persons…and newborn babies are other persons.

THE DOUBLE STANDARD

Franklin Zimring, professor of law at the University of California-Berkeley, points out how accepting low-income adolescent parenthood while encouraging middle-class adolescents to terminate pregnancies or create adoption plans reveals a double standard. Ageism, sexism and racism are all contributing factors as pointed out previously in this book.

Most adolescents who become pregnant realize that it is unwise to enter parenthood. But this wisdom often is not reinforced by their families, professionals or society. To deprive adolescents of informed consent—the most important part of which is to ensure that they fully understand the responsibilities and consequences of parenthood—is an abrogation of parental and professional obligations. It violates the responsibility of professionals to do no harm.

Title XX of the Public Health Service Act specifies necessary services for Adolescent Family Life Demonstration Projects. These include adoption counseling and referral services; education on the responsibilities of sexuality and parenting; and counseling for immediate and extended family members. This model should be available to all pregnant adolescents and their families as proposed in the next chapter.

THE INTERESTS OF SOCIETY

Our society generally regards preventing teen pregnancy as an important priority. Adolescent pregnancy doesn't stop being a social and personal crisis when a baby is born. Adolescent parenthood is an even greater crisis with additional health, welfare and legal entanglements.

From society's point of view, should adolescent childbirth be approached reactively with damage control that might amplify its effects or thoughtfully with holistic planning that can dampen its effects? We have enough knowledge and opportunities to prevent damage if we connect adolescent parenthood to social problems. We don't need to feel helpless when an adolescent girl gives birth. We can apply the knowledge and problem-solving skills we already have.

Articulating cultural values that discourage premature sexual intercourse and parenthood can dramatically change adolescent behavior. Our country had success with this method in the early Twentieth Century, and the same success is evident in other countries today. The media's contemporary promotion of sexual behavior could be counteracted by a public health campaign highlighting the disadvantages of adolescent sexual intercourse and pregnancy just like those mounted against smoking, drug abuse and drunk driving. Civic groups, churches and celebrities could articulate standards for sexual behavior and parenthood just as they have to promote educational achievement. Mayor Michael Bloomberg initiated a teen pregnancy prevention campaign in New York City in March of 2013. As might be expected, it stirred up criticism reflecting juvenile ageism that treats adolescent parents as adults and that ignores the right of newborn babies to have competent parents.

THE INTERESTS OF ADOLESCENTS

Generally a genetic parent is in the best position to raise a child. This principle guides family preservation in social work. It's affirmed by fetus-mother bonding throughout pregnancy and by breastfeeding after childbirth. But possessing the judgment, skills and economic resources for parenthood is more important than the ability to conceive, give birth and breastfeed. Genetic mothers and fathers who recognize they don't possess these qualities make adoption plans.

In 1983, Marie Winn called attention to children who were growing up without childhoods. This is even more prevalent today. One symptom of the denigration of parenthood is the private and public support offered adolescent parents. It presumes that young people who can't handle the responsibilities of their own lives can handle the responsibilities of parenthood despite our increasingly complicated world.

If we recognize adolescence as a developmental stage and if we define parenthood as an adult responsibility, we can restore childhood for children and adolescence for adolescents. Our society must realize that it can't cut short the years of nurturing and protection its young need by allowing them to assume adult responsibilities prematurely in any venue.

We need to understand that the developmental characteristics of adolescence and the influences, or the lack thereof, of parents cause more adolescent pregnancies than ignorance and socioeconomic disadvantage. Antipoverty measures alone don't address parent-child relationships. In their book *A Mentor, Peer Group, Incentive Model for Helping Underclass Youth*, Ronald Mincy and Susan Weiner noted that poverty is less important than the parents' behavior in influencing an adolescent girl's chance of becoming pregnant.

Most importantly, we need to recognize that the charitable impulse to support adolescent parents can have unintended consequences. We need to shift from damage control to offering hope and empowerment.

State statutes use age-grading to protect minors from activities beyond their abilities as well as to protect society from minor's inappropriate actions. Valuing parenthood enough to set minimum standards could be a tipping point that shifts our society from self-assertive values to integrative cultural values. The most important issue facing us today is whether we value children and our nation's future enough to value parenthood as a career for adults who can handle its responsibilities.

Governmental Interventions in Family Life

If every citizen respected the rights of others, we wouldn't need law enforcement. We wouldn't need welfare if every individual was capable of, and had the opportunity to, lead an economically self-sufficient life. Unfortunately, everyone does not have these qualities or opportunities. We will always need law enforcement and some form of welfare.

We will always face the repercussions of incompetent parents if we do not set standards for parenthood. Currently, all parents are assumed to be competent until they damage their children by neglect or abuse. A more accurate assumption is that the vast majority of parents are competent but children and society need protection from the millions who are not.

We cannot assume competence in parenting any more than we can assume competence in any other activity that affects others. Licensing is intended to ensure that persons who do important things for others are competent and responsible. Irresponsible people conceive and bear children. For this reason, children and society now could have protection from incompetent parents by refining the prevention provisions of child neglect and abuse statutes. When parents are unable or unwilling to become competent, these statutes currently require that parental rights be terminated and the children be adopted.

Parents' abdication of their responsibilities necessitated laws that mandate parental participation in school conferences; the liability of grandparents for the children of their children; the liability of non-custodial parents for financial support; and the liability of parents for their children's actions. However, because of the subtle but powerful juvenile ageist assumption that children are property, a belief concealed by the emphasis on family privacy and individual freedom, we intervene only after children have been damaged by their parents.

If all parents were competent, the government wouldn't need to be involved in family life. Because the neglect, abuse and exploitation of children damage the next generation and create financial burdens for the present generation, government has a clear-cut role in preventing neglect and abuse by setting standards for parenthood. All of us are paying an ever-larger share of the cost of rearing, educating and treating children. Consequently, we all have a financial stake in preventing child neglect and abuse.

Around the world, governments are defining and regulating parenthood in response to conflicts between adult rights and children's needs. Underlying those conflicts is the erosion of the nuclear family. Children also are increasingly being viewed as commodities in the IVF and adoption

marketplaces. A new paradigm is needed. The assumption that anyone regardless of age or capacity has legal and physical custodianship until a child
is damaged must be challenged.

Our standards for responsible adulthood include supporting yourself
legally and abiding by society's laws and regulations. Standards are set for
foster parents, adoptive parents, divorce custody and visitation arrangements, childcare, preschools, schools and others who are responsible for
children's lives. Minimum standards for parenthood would protect children from neglect and abuse and all of us from the consequences. Standards
won't create optimal childrearing scenarios but will identify the worst scenarios. What's good for children may be controversial but what's bad for
them is not as is clearly outlined in our child neglect and abuse laws.

Too many of our children are growing up in families that prevent them
from becoming responsible, productive citizens. The repetitive cycle of adolescent and dependent adult parents followed by child abuse and neglect
is the most preventable source of habitual crime and welfare dependency.

Our society needs a paradigm shift from our dominant self-assertive
social values toward integrative cultural values. We can protect our nation's
future by ensuring that all children have competent parents. We would
then value parenthood as a career with as much economic and social value
as paid employment. Parents would be able to compete economically with
adults without children.

Because our society doesn't articulate expectations for parents, child
neglect and abuse have reached epidemic proportions. Rates in the United
States exceed that of all other developed nations. We only intervene after
neglect and abuse have occurred, and often then ineffectively. Enormous
public expenditures on treatment, rehabilitation and incarceration result.
This would change dramatically if our vision for America was that all our
children will be raised by competent parents.

By failing to recognize a newborn baby's right to competent parents
with adequate resources, our society will continue to be anti-child and anti-
parent. If we go on this way, we will ensure that America continues to decline. By addressing the basic needs of families, we can correct our course
one child and one parent at a time. We need a system that sets standards for
parenthood and that includes in-home and community guidance for new

parents along with ensuring that all families have adequate family resource systems.

WHAT DO WE KNOW?

Two vital aspects of parenthood are often overlooked. The first is that readiness for parenthood follows the adolescent stage of life. The ability to assume responsibility for one's own life is a prerequisite for assuming responsibility for the life of another person. The second is that parenthood is a developmental stage in life. Parents progress though egocentric, conventional, individualistic and integrative phases of parenthood.

Controversies arise over whether pregnancy and childbirth themselves promote maturity; whether everyone has a right to parenthood regardless of age; and whether genetic parents are always the best person to raise a child. In the past, preparation for parenthood occurred within families. With loosening family ties and family strife in the United States, preparation for parenthood now often must come from educational and clinical sources.

By entering parenthood, adolescents gain financial benefits in the form of Temporary Assistance for Needy Families, Medicaid, counseling, educational accommodations, and childcare in addition to increased status with their peers and possibly families. Adoption is not appealing because it means parting with their babies and these benefits. Making an adoption plan also might evoke disapproval from relatives and peers. All these factors encourage adolescents to become parents despite the likelihood of unfavorable outcomes.

The best time for decision-making about parenthood and adoption plans is when a pregnancy first becomes known. The more mature adolescent parents are, the more likely they will choose not to enter parenthood. The overall evidence indicates that children who were adopted as babies fare as well as children reared in genetic families.

To ensure that children have competent parents, parenthood must be recognized as a developmental stage that follows adolescence and as an essential complement to childhood. Struggling parents also need access to collaborative systems of care, the topic of the next chapter.

Chapter Twelve

Overcoming Our Crisis-Recoil Response

*The most important measure of any society is not the
standard that its strongest members set for themselves, but
rather where they fix the moral bar for the weaker.*

KAY S. HYMOWITZ
MARRIAGE AND CASTE IN AMERICA

Anthropologist Margaret Mead eloquently called attention to the damaging institutional response to children when they are treated as independent persons during crises. Since most crisis interventions occur *after* rather than *before* damage occurs, children frequently are victims of crisis-recoil responses in which an overreaction to crises in their lives is followed by recoiling from the causes of the crises.

CRISIS-RECOIL POLITICAL RESPONSE

Our crisis-recoil political system overreacts to crises and then ignores their causes. This avoids responsibility for making difficult decisions. As a result, there's little or no emphasis on prevention or concern about the future impact of current actions. Because of our crisis-recoil political response, we react to child neglect and abuse without addressing their underlying causes.

This is seen when children are removed from their homes during a crisis as if they were independent persons rather than recognizing their dependence on their parents. This response often includes little to strengthen their families. Later, the inevitable shortage of foster homes is dealt with by seeking more foster homes and raising reimbursement for them rather than by addressing the family problems that necessitated so many foster homes in the first place.

Public policies fail to recognize that a child is half of a two-person unit that depends on the integrity of the mediating structures of family, neighborhood, school and community. Child protective services only intervene when families break down. As a result, services that focus on individual children and that fragment families have been overdeveloped while resources that support parenthood and community building have been underdeveloped. Shirley Johnson's family described in Chapter One of this book is a typical example.

Another obvious example is our response to and punishment of criminal behavior. Police intervene after crimes have been committed, and more prisons are built in the belief that the penal system will solve the social problem of crime. Punishment of crime becomes a reality-avoidance mechanism that recoils from the underlying causes. Punishment of a culprit permits the public to believe that the crisis created by a crime has been resolved.

The crisis-recoil phenomenon is illustrated further by regulations that mandate medical treatment for grossly defective newborns. The response to the crisis at birth is to save the child's life. Recoil from the cause of the newborn's crisis and its repercussions means there's no assessment of the impact of preserving the newborn's life and no provision for treatment after the child leaves the intensive-care neonatal unit. The child remains dependent on expensive technology to maintain physical life often to the disruption and potential financial ruin of the family.

The lack of appreciation of the importance of family ties also is highlighted in the crisis-recoil management of divorce custody and visitation matters. After the crisis of divorce has subsided, the lack of access to their children makes parents aware of how important their children are to them. They recoil through custody contests that usually are harmful to their children.

The crisis-recoil nature of our political and human services systems only aggravates our social problems. We need to strengthen the mediating structures that can solve those problems by more clearly articulating cultural values that support family, neighborhood and community relationships. We can do this by applying the basic principles of public health.

THREE KINDS OF PREVENTION OF SOCIAL PROBLEMS

The public health concepts of primary, secondary and tertiary prevention can be profitably applied to social problems. *Primary prevention* is the prevention of a disease or harm. *Secondary prevention* treats a disease or harm. *Tertiary prevention* manages and minimizes disability from the disease or harm. As it stands now, our social, educational and mental health services are oriented largely to secondary and tertiary prevention, as the following examples indicate.

Primary Prevention

Home visitation programs for the parents of newborns are available in many communities. They offer both prenatal and natal services designed to strengthen families on both a request and referral basis. Healthy Families America is an example of a nationally recognized evidence-based home visiting program model designed to work with overburdened families who are at-risk for adverse childhood experiences, including child maltreatment.

The premier neighborhood organization Harlem Children's Zone, Inc., (HCZ) began in 1970 as Rheedlen. HCZ worked with young children and their families as the city's first truancy-prevention program. In the early 1990s, it ran a pilot project that brought a range of support services to a single block. The idea was to address all the problems that disadvantaged families faced from crumbling apartments to failing schools and from violent crime to chronic health problems. In 1997, the agency began a network of programs for a twenty-four block area. In 2007, the Zone Project grew to almost 100 blocks. Today the HCZ serves more than 8,000 children and 6,000 adults.

In North Carolina, the East Durham Children's Initiative is an example of efforts around the country to replicate the Harlem Children's Zone. In

Omaha, Nebraska, Building Bright Futures sponsors school-based health centers and offers mentoring and enrichment services.

Secondary Prevention

The Strengthening Families Program was developed in the early 1980s by Karol Kumpfer. Its fourteen sessions cover child development, behavior management, child skills training, family skills enhancement and attachment bonding and psycho-educational material targeted at improving the child-parent relationship. Currently it is being used with struggling families in every state and in seventeen nations. It results in higher rates of family reunification than traditional methods.

Secondary and Tertiary Prevention

Collaborative Systems of Care provide integrated support and resources for struggling families in a collaborative, family-centered way that leads to better outcomes for individuals, families and communities. They also reduce duplication of effort and are an effective use of limited resources.

Coordinated Services/Wraparound Teams

Wraparound/Coordinated Services Teams emerged in the early 1980s as a collaborative planning approach to community-based care for children and youth with complex mental health and related challenges. These teams are promoted and monitored by the National Wraparound Initiative. A wraparound team brings together family members, service and resource providers and people from the family's social support network. Team members create, implement and monitor a plan to meet family needs.

Wraparound planning focuses on meeting the needs and reaching the goals that family members identify as most essential. The Wraparound process is individualized, culturally competent, strength based and outcome oriented.

Each Wraparound site has a coordinating committee made up of parents and representatives from agencies and organizations that serve children and families. The committee's responsibilities include:

- Developing policies and procedures, including an inter-agency service agreement;

- Developing and implementing a plan for sustainability; and

- Evaluation and quality assurance, including family and provider satisfaction.

Wraparound teams have four phases of involvement: 1) strengths and needs assessment; 2) an individualized plan of care based on identified strengths and needs, including crisis response plans for home, school and community; 3) ongoing monitoring of the plan with the support of team members; and 4) plans for transition from the formal team process to ensure the family has a voice in decisions, access to resources and ownership of their achievements.

Multisystemic Therapy

Multisystemic Therapy (MST) is an intensive family-community-based treatment program that focuses on the world of chronic and violent juvenile offenders—their homes, schools and neighborhoods. MST works with adolescents between the ages of twelve and seventeen who have arrest histories. The MST team of several therapists is intensively involved with families through at least three home visits a week and is available by telephone 24/7 for eleven to thirty weeks. MST has been applied in the United States and at least seven other countries.

THE PRIMARY PREVENTION OF DEPENDENT PARENTHOOD

Current child welfare interventions focus on secondary prevention with dependent parents. The hope is that they won't neglect or abuse their babies and that subsequent births will be prevented. The emphasis needs to be shifted to the primary prevention of dependent parenthood. Child neglect and abuse statutes already allow termination of parental rights at childbirth when circumstances warrant, including the absence of a competent parent. These statutes can specifically address the unavailability of a qualified legal and physical custodian. In order to function effectively, child welfare workers need this kind of support from legislation.

Our public health system is devoted to preventing physical, mental and social disorders. The system promotes education, advocacy, services and enforcement guided by legislation. In addition, the Child Abuse Prevention and Treatment Act of 1974 placed the moral weight of the federal government behind professional interventions to help struggling families.

As public health knowledge about preventable conditions emerges, legislation is enacted. Examples include mandated immunization of school children and testing at birth for phenylketonuria, a treatable predisposition to mental and neurological disorders. The Keeping Children and Families Safe Act of 2003 requires states to ensure that health care providers report babies affected by prenatal drug exposure to child protective services.

Many states have gone further. Physicians in New Jersey are required to educate expectant mothers about postpartum depression and screen new mothers for it. HIV testing of pregnant women is mandatory in some states because protecting the unborn child supersedes the mother's right to refuse testing. These measures are precedents for legislation on the crisis of adolescent childbirth.

The international response to the H1N1 flu epidemic of 2009 illustrates how national leadership can galvanize action when we know the nature of a problem and what to do about. Modern public health, which quickly recognizes changes in the course of an illness and pours out resources to prevent it, shows our ability to plan and take action when we decide to do so.

A flu epidemic is far less important to our nation's wellbeing and our leadership in the world economy than the birth of babies who are destined to fail in life and cause the majority of our social problems. We know what the problem is and what to do about it, but we lack the national leadership and the political will to apply what we know and to act.

Health care underwent a paradigm shift when our focus on treating the disabilities caused by poliomyelitis shifted to preventing polio through immunization. Dentistry underwent a paradigm shift when we shifted the focus from treating dental caries to preventing it through fluoridation of our water supply. Human services are beginning a paradigm shift from protecting children by removing them from their homes to strengthening their families. Unfortunately, the next paradigm shift to ensuring that newborns have competent parents is obstructed by juvenile ageism that objects to government invasion of the privacy of families and restriction of the freedom of parents to do as they wish with their children. As a result, we ignore newborns' most basic need for parents who can provide adequate care for them and don't enact the legislation needed to fill that need.

GOVERNMENTAL POWER VS. INDIVIDUAL RIGHTS

For good reason, we restrict the government's power to intervene in private lives to circumstances in which serious harm to others or society is likely. When people abuse their freedom to act, the challenge is to identify situations that warrant legal intervention. The freedom to procreate and raise children is among our most cherished rights. Any limitation of this right will understandably prove to be controversial. Nonetheless, our laws clearly state that parents are *not* free to neglect or abuse their children.

In 1977 in *Carey v. Population Services International*, the U.S. Supreme Court noted "the incidence of sexual activity among minors is high, and the consequences of such activity are frequently devastating...." This recognition especially when minors already have limited legal privileges opens the door to an *in loco parentis* role for the state whenever a dependent minor chooses to continue a pregnancy to childbirth.

In legal terms, being a minor is a disability. The gradual achievement of adult independence is the process of outgrowing the *disability of infancy*. Our age-grading laws recognize that adolescents are incapable of making life-altering decisions. Progressively awarding adult privileges protects a youth's healthy development and safety.

Driver training and graduated licensing programs, for example, significantly reduce fatalities among young drivers. The Safe Teen and Novice Driver Uniform Protection Act of 2011 (H.R. 1515) would create a National Graduated Driver Licensing law that limits night driving, reduces in-car distractions, puts a cap on the number of friends in the car and increases the required hours of training and supervision. This kind of age-grading principle should apply to parenthood as well. This federal Act was not adopted in 2011 or 2012 on the grounds that it is a state issue.

Unfortunately legal traditions have followed outdated common law that fails to recognize adolescence as a developmental stage. Adolescent immaturity is ignored when parental rights and legal emancipation are granted to minors. These traditions both view adolescence as a temporary status rather than a stage of development and ignore the fact that the first weeks and months of a baby's life are crucial periods that have profound and lasting consequences.

Often adolescent parents need double protection from their own incompetence as parents as well as from that of their parents. Their babies need protection from their young parents as well as from their extended family. To ensure that both adolescents and their babies receive competent parenting, we need a more realistic way to view the legal status of the babies of adolescent parents.

NEWBORNS NEED COMPETENT CUSTODIANS

At the beginning and possibly at the end of life, a human being requires a legal and physical custodian or guardian. When the elderly are no longer competent to make decisions and manage their own lives, states enable relatives to take over as conservators for their finances and health care. We have no problem accepting the need for state involvement in the affairs of incompetent adults. We do have difficulty accepting the same need at the beginning of life when state involvement is even more critical. The future holds newborn persons' entire lives, not their deaths.

Fortunately, when the rights of children and parents conflict, the evolving legal trend is to place children's interests first. A baby's interests rise above the wishes of her or his dependent parents and their families. In fact, the babies of dependent minors and adults don't have legal and physical custodians capable of:

- Ensuring they receive nurturance and life's material necessities.

- Making prudent decisions concerning their welfare and wellbeing.

- Arranging for and authorizing health care.

- Advocating their interests.

In some states, antiquated laws regard childbirth as an act that emancipates minors from their parents' authority. Nevertheless, minors cannot be legal and physical custodians of their babies, a reality recognized whenever a court appoints a guardian *ad litem* (an officer of the court) to represent a minor parent in adoption proceedings. Simply put, minors cannot be legal and physical custodians of other persons *because they require legal and physical custodians themselves.*

The age-grading principle built into our laws prevents minors from assuming responsibility for the life of another person. Their brain development and their emotional and social maturity don't enable them to make decisions that permanently affect their own lives let alone those of their babies.

Right now, grandparents can have statutory financial liability for a grandchild's support but not legal or physical custodianship. They and other supportive family members need to be released from this trap. Some states now permit *de facto* custodianship when minor parents default on the care of their children to adult relatives, but this is too little, too late.

The adolescent childbirth crisis now evokes a number of interventions ranging from paternity determination to group home placement for mother and baby. These interventions often span months or years while the baby's interests are neglected. We must view adolescent childbirth from the newborn baby's point of view. We need a vision in which the birth of every baby is a cause for celebration of a new person's opportunity to succeed in our nation.

When it is clear that this will not be the case, we need to bring a baby's birth as close as possible to this vision. Because adolescent childbirth is a public health crisis masked by powerful emotions, we need to use existing health, social welfare and legal resources when a minor's pregnancy is first identified. We also need to establish best practices to ensure that an unborn baby's interests come first. To reach this goal, we can start by implementing the primary prevention provisions of our child neglect and abuse statutes that apply to newborns who will not have a qualified parent...a legal and physical custodian. As has been made clear previously, the newborn babies of dependent persons do not have qualified legal and physical custodians.

The present stance of intervening only after children are damaged is inhumane and costly. This can be remedied by mandating Parenthood Planning Counseling for all pregnant minors and dependent adults that includes their custodians. We need to craft legal and clinical procedures to deal with the fact that both adolescent mothers and fathers and their babies require protection. Resolving critical parenthood issues before birth is the single most important step we can take to reduce crime and welfare dependency in our nation.

PARENTHOOD PLANNING COUNSELING

Health care professionals are key to Parenthood Planning Counseling for pregnant girls, dependent women, dependent fathers, and their families. Title XX of the Public Health Service Act already requires that Adolescent Family Life Demonstration Projects include this counseling that includes the minor's family to address the option of adoption and the responsibilities of sexuality and parenting. In this context, the following programs can offer or arrange for Parenthood Planning Counseling:

- Family planning and health care clinics that provide pregnancy diagnosis

- Medicaid Prenatal Care Coordination services

- Prenatal care clinics

- Prenatal home visitation programs

Within these programs, professionals can approach dependent pregnant mothers and their families with open minds. The goal is to develop a shared understanding of concerns, priorities, strengths and challenges, always with sensitivity to cultural factors. To this end, materials are available to assist counseling with black, Latino, American Indian and southeastern Asian families, such as provided by the Center for the Improvement of Child Caring.

When it occurs, pregnancy usually represents the first life-altering decision of a girl's life. She and the baby's father when involved can be expected to be uncertain about what to do. Most adolescents have little if any counseling about their options in managing their pregnancies. Along with facts and reassurance, they need help exploring their fantasies, fears, anxieties, guilt and hopes. The adolescent's parents might express their guilt through anger toward or support of the pregnant girl and the father. All parties need to explore their feelings about the pregnancy.

It is important to know that many girls embrace pregnancy to avoid isolation and loneliness. Many fear facing their feelings of emptiness and inadequacy and seek the love of a baby. Abandonment by their fathers often accentuates these feelings. The resulting despair and unworthiness can result in unwise decisions.

Ideally decisions regarding the course of a pregnancy should be made when pregnancy is diagnosed, and its existence is accepted by all concerned. This is the most clearheaded time to consider everyone's interests…those of the unborn child, mother, father, their families and society.

Discovering a pregnancy is an emotional event. Still, the physical and emotional changes of advanced pregnancy and childbirth have not yet occurred. The potential mother and father and their families therefore are in the best position to fully weigh the pros and cons of each possible course. If the decision is to continue the pregnancy, the interests of the newborn baby should move to the forefront. This provides five to seven months to work through guilt, shame, pride and fantasies about childrearing…and to plan for adoption at birth if that is the best course.

If a decision is postponed, the hormonal and physical changes of late pregnancy cloud objective thinking. After childbirth, prolactin and oxytocin activate instincts that motivate mothers to strongly attach to their babies. Pitressin produces similar responses in fathers. This is the time when objective decision making is the least likely to occur.

Consummating the decision-making process during pregnancy also is critical for the wellbeing of the newborn. The first weeks and months of a baby's life have profound developmental consequences, especially for the attachment bonding process. The compelling interests of the newborn should take precedence over the traditional view that mothers and fathers need time after birth to decide about adoption.

PARENTHOOD PLANNING TEAMS

The existing prevention provisions of child neglect and abuse statutes are the basis for Parenthood Planning Counseling through Parenthood Planning Teams. Public health practices like case reporting, counseling and law enforcement can be used to implement counseling for all adolescent parents. Currently these interventions are mandated only in cases where child neglect or abuse is suspected.

A Parenthood Planning Team would, depending on individual circumstances, consist of two or more of the following: a family planning counselor, prenatal care counselor, or public health nurse; a child welfare worker to implement the guardianship petition process; other professionals involved with the adolescent or her family; and when appropriate, a guardian *ad litem*. The potential for this kind of teamwork exists now in prenatal home visitation, prenatal care coordination and Wraparound/Coordinated Services Teams.

A Parenthood Planning Team would be activated whenever parenthood is on the horizon for minors or adults with developmental disabilities, previous termination of parental rights or incarceration as violent felons or domestic abusers. These categories need to be considered individually with a focus on the interests of everyone involved.

In addition the criteria for incarceration need to be revised. Most of the 84,000 women in federal and state prisons are serving a year or less for possession or trafficking in illegal substances, shoplifting, bad checks or stolen credit cards. Of those in Illinois, most are in their thirties with three or four children; 63% are high school drop-outs; 60% have substance abuse problems; 85% are single mothers; and most are victims of domestic abuse. We need to shift their sentencing from incarceration to community management so that their families are not disrupted. Then they can receive the help they need through Collaborative Systems of Care, such as Wraparound/Coordinated Services Teams.

We need to consider the life circumstances and abilities of each parent in order to identify the most appropriate options. Because each parent's situation is unique, a Parenthood Planning Team would determine the most appropriate course of action. Just as a patient's capacity to give informed consent for health care must be evaluated, the team must evaluate a minor parent's decision-making capacities for entering parenthood or adoption.

SHORT-TERM DESIRES AND LONG-TERM INTERESTS

Most of us understand that we should eat reasonably, live within our means, avoid addictions, be sexually responsible, keep promises and hold undesirable impulses in check. Yet we regularly violate at least some of these tenets...not because we want to harm ourselves but because we fail to control our urges. Most importantly, pop culture often glorifies self-indulgent and self-defeating actions..."just do it."

In this ambivalent social atmosphere, pregnant girls, conceiving boys and dependent adults need Parenthood Planning Counseling along with their parents. This counseling is vital for making decisions that place the interests of the newborn baby first followed by those of the adolescents, their families and society.

Such counseling should *not* be based on either supporting the status quo or satisfying individual desires. It should be focused on the aim of productive citizenship for adolescents and dependent adults as well as for their newborn babies. It places long-term interests ahead of short-term desires.

Most adolescents and dependent adults who become pregnant have difficulty envisioning the alternatives and consequences. They need guidance in identifying their babies' and their own self-interests along with the consequences of their choices. They need to understand the responsibilities of parenthood. They need to fully realize that a baby is not a possession but a human being entitled to competent parenting. They need to fully realize the impact of imposing the burdens of childrearing on their parents and relatives. They need to realistically understand adoption.

Young people also need help understanding that adolescence is an important life stage that will be shortchanged by parenthood's physical, emotional, psychological and economic consequences. A girl needs to understand that parenthood exposes her and her child to elevated risks of poverty, inadequate education, depression, welfare dependency and prison. Even with financial benefits, parenthood will not eliminate disadvantaged circumstances.

We need to create opportunities and language for sharing our knowledge about the best interests of a child so that young people can make these life-altering decisions.

Chapter Thirteen

In the Best Interests of Children and Adolescents

...the future of a society may be forecast by the way it cares for its young.

DANIEL PATRICK MOYNIHAN, 1986
NATIONAL COMMISSION ON CHILDREN, 1991

The deepest human bond is between mother and child. It has a sacred aura. Our instinctive response to mother and her newborn baby is awe and empathy. We view her baby as her own flesh and blood even though the fetus actually was not a part of her body. This response underlies the legal framework that protects family privacy and parental rights. It also means that the image of a baby as a mother's possession can override recognition that a newborn is a separate human being. As a result, the question of "true mother love" is seldom raised today, as it was in the proverbial wisdom of Solomon:

> Two women claimed the same child as their own. Solomon offered to cut the baby in half to settle the dispute. One woman replied she would rather forfeit the child than see him killed. Solomon judged her to be the true child's mother and awarded her the child.

The core of assessing a mother's love is whether that love is self or baby oriented. Does she view her baby as her possession or her responsibility? Does she see herself as an owner or a custodian of her baby? Which is foremost: what her baby can do for her or what she can do for her baby? In essence is the baby's purpose to fulfill her desires or to develop as an autonomous person?

These questions must be raised with adolescents and dependent adults as they consider continuing a pregnancy to childbirth. Are their motives egocentric or centered on the best interests of the unborn child? Although the phrase "in the best interests of the child" is commonly used, too often the phrase "the least detrimental alternative" more accurately describes a given situation. Still our focus now is on the best interests of the newborn baby and the adolescent parent.

Enhancing an Adolescent's Personal Growth

Approaching pregnancy with a problem-solving attitude can enhance an adolescent's personal growth. Adolescents can learn how to question and resolve their egocentric desires and gain self-respect and self-confidence in doing so.

Adolescence is a critical time for learning how to resolve personal problems in ways that uncover and serve true self-interests. Self-fulfillment can't occur without growth in awareness, knowledge, wisdom and long-term planning. Deferring individual wishes and urges for the benefit of others is character building. When adolescents acknowledge that becoming pregnant unintentionally or intentionally was a mistake, they can make decisions that avoid grave consequences for everyone.

The decision-making process can be particularly crucial for dependent persons who are in a position to reverse intergenerational cycles of academic and social failure. They need help seeing that, contrary to their predecessors, they can build self-respect and self-confidence through achievements other than childbirth. They can be empowered to face and master the challenges of adolescence without the responsibilities of parenthood.

Involving Families

A dependent mother's family is crucial to the course of her pregnancy and its aftermath. A family can choose to assist in childrearing. However, this can be complicated by an adolescent parent's mental and emotional problems. Family members shouldn't assume responsibilities for a dependent mother's baby without having the decision-making authority accorded by legal and physical custodianship of the baby.

Even then, parents of dependent parents can't be presumed to be competent. Parental involvement might not be desirable when incest, abuse, alcoholism or drug abuse is involved. Intervention might be necessary to obtain a legal and physical custodian for the dependent mother herself and for her baby. A Parenthood Planning Team can assess whether or not relatives are capable of assuming childrearing responsibilities for a dependent mother and for her baby.

Adoption Planning

Prior to the 1970s, adoption was the most frequent outcome of adolescent childbirth in the United States. Now it seldom occurs. Still, the process of adoption through an agency comes as close to assuring parental competence as any method currently available. Contrary to what many people believe, adoptive parents are available for babies born in the United States as indicated by the large volume of international adoptions. Barriers to transracial adoption are no longer significant.

Still, the word *adoption* can evoke a variety of emotions sadness over separating children from their genetic parents; fear of placing children in strange families; shame and guilt for resorting to adoption; and anger at professionals who might seem to treat children as commodities. The process also can evoke gratitude and affection in adoptive parents, in adopted children and in genetic parents who have seen their children thrive in adoptive homes. A mixture of these feelings is common.

Adoption commonly is viewed as providing children for parents who want them. A more appropriate view is *providing competent parents for children who need them* as psychiatrist Denis Donovan shows in *The Choice Model: A Values-Based Logic-Driven Approach to Adoption.* A child-centered view focuses on the needs of children. Children's needs for parents are far more important than adults' needs for children. Adults can thrive without children. Children cannot thrive without competent parents.

Babies adopted at birth have the genes of their conceiving parents along with prenatal and postnatal interactions with genetic mothers. But their personalities have not yet formed. They don't have reciprocal attachment bonds with anyone and have no family identity. Their first reciprocal attachment bonds are with the parents who adopt them...their *real parents*. They are the real children of their real parents. They haven't lost their identity or been saddled with unresolved emotions.

The Mystique of Blood Relationships

The popular assumption is that blood ties are the deepest and most enduring of all human relationships. Parents and children love each other because they share the same genes. Adopted children presumably seek their biological parents because of a genetically determined attraction. In fact even when parent-child ties have genetic proclivities, their depth is determined by life experiences. The strongest human bond is between a genetic mother and child because of the bond's experiential basis rather than because of genes.

The mutual affection shared by genetically related persons is based on their relationships. Some adopted children and stepchildren have gone through life believing they were their parents' genetic offspring. They didn't suffer adverse consequences.

Without DNA testing, fathers have no definitive way to determine parentage other than what they believe to be true. The perception of being blood relatives defines their relationships, not the actual sharing of genes. Babies do not connect with their genetic fathers unless interaction creates an affiliative father-child bond. A father's reaction to discovering that a child is or is not his own also is based on his perceptions rather than his genes.

Babies and children form reciprocal attachment bonds with parents who interact with them. Children who discover they were adopted react to that information but they don't shift their bonding relationships from adoptive parents to genetic parents. Their reactions are determined by their experiences and their attachment bonds.

Genes are designed to take their cues from nurture. The more we lift the lid on the human genome, the more we see how strongly genes are influenced by experience. Life experience is the basis for parenthood, not genes.

Negative Attitudes toward Adoption

Neuroscience suggests that when people must choose between a risky outcome and an uncertain one, the tendency is to make the risky choice. This is especially true for adolescents.

For high-risk adolescents, short-term incentives for becoming parents outweigh long-term incentives for not entering parenthood. They gain financial benefits, counseling, educational accommodations, childcare and even status with families and peers. The prospect of adoption is unappealing because they must part with their babies and they might possibly evoke disapproval from families and peers.

Adoption bears a stigma despite decades of experience that proves its benefits for children, genetic parents, adopting parents and society. As the social stigma of unwed pregnancy and single parenthood diminished, young mothers became more reluctant to make adoption plans. This is especially true if their families are willing to help with childrearing and financial support and are guided by beliefs like the following.

Adoption is Irresponsible

The negative aura of adoption might be fueled by the belief that a genetic mother and father must enter parenthood and take responsibility for their actions. This belief compromises a genetic parent's education, social life, career and financial independence. It adds the burden of childrearing to their families. It makes adoption a shameful choice for a girl and possibly for a boy, especially when this belief is shared by their families and peers.

Adoption as Abandonment

Making an adoption plan might be considered child abandonment. Families and peers therefore might criticize the choice at the time. An adopted child, this belief claims, might grow up to feel betrayed by the genetic mother.

Irreparable Wounds

The depth of feeling evoked by adoption is poignantly revealed in this blog:

> I am one of the millions of mothers and children of adoption wounds. Many of us are sick or dying young from the grief of having our children taken from us by adoption brokers. Only in America will a community tell a mother and adopted person that have lost each other to coercion to be grateful. Adopted persons and mothers have committed suicide due to the trauma of adoption. Many adopted teens are in treatment centers.

A radical feminist view on the adolescent baby adoption prevalent in prior decades states:

> In the past, experts recommended that the girl and her family must arrange her disappearance from the community. Then the unwed mother must undergo intensive psychological treatment; and most important, she must agree to relinquish her illegitimate child to a married couple, for without a husband, the young woman was not a mother, according to the ideology of the era.

> Maternity homes were considered a reform over the days when "fallen women" were stigmatized. The new, professionalized staff rarely imagined the devastating, lifelong consequences many unwed mothers of that era suffered for having been shamed and coerced into relinquishing their babies.

Fortunately, these views do not reflect the experience of the vast majority of people who make adoption plans. The separation involved in adoption doesn't cause mental illness. The event of adoption often is incorrectly used to explain unrelated, often pre-existing, emotional and psychological problems of mothers who make adoption plans.

Open Adoptions

Open adoption has become the dominant form because genetic parents find it attractive. Since it is a relatively recent practice, little is known about its long-term outcomes.

AAA Partners in Adoption, Inc., offers free Parenthood Planning Counseling and emotional support during pregnancy, at delivery and after birth. The agency approves families waiting for children. Genetic parents can receive assistance with medical care and living expenses. A counselor helps the genetic mother relinquish her rights to the child so that adoption can proceed. The baby usually goes home from the hospital with the adopting family. In Georgia, the genetic father receives notice of the adoption. If his cooperation cannot be secured, his parental rights are terminated at no cost to the mother.

Impact on the Children

At one end of a continuum stand children who were adopted early in life and whose lives are the same as those of children raised by genetic parents. At the other end are those who suffered the consequences of deprivations and disruptions before their adoption later in life.

Adoption is an issue for most children. Most young children, including those who have been adopted, experience the "family romance" fantasy. They imagine they have different, usually idealized, parents. For an adopted child, this fantasy can idealize the genetic parents. How much of a child's response to adoption is based on a family romance fantasy and how much is based on the adoption might be difficult to separate. Children who were adopted commonly raise the following questions:

- Why was I not wanted by my genetic parents?

- How did my parents get me?

- Will my parents keep me no matter what?

These children might feel the stigma of adoption. But with the support of their parents, most cope with those feelings. Some build a unique identity more fully than children who weren't adopted.

Adoption is preferable to other options such as institutional rearing, foster care or incompetent genetic parents. A child's pre-adoptive experience, age at placement, family dynamics and demographic factors determine the outcomes of adoption. The following generalizations have been made about children who were adopted:

- The vast majority do not have significant adjustment problems.

- They have far less behavioral and psychological problems, less adolescent pregnancies and higher educational attainment than those in similar circumstances at birth who were not adopted.

- Those not adopted as newborns are at somewhat higher risk of having school-related behavioral and psychological problems than children raised in two-parent genetic families. These issues are often attributed to genetic factors and adversity earlier in their lives prior to adoption.

- They might struggle to make sense of issues raised by adoption especially during middle childhood when children are trying to understand their lives.

Adoption as a Sacrifice

The prospect of separating a mother and her family from a baby runs counter to the natural intent of reproduction. Relatives of the mother and father also experience pride and affection for the baby. They view the child as a possession that extends down the family line. No wonder mature judgment and courage are required for any mother to make an adoption plan.

For pregnant adolescents the choice is simple: *to enter parenthood or not to enter parenthood.* This shifts the focus from the baby to the real-world obligations of parenthood, from the idea of being a parent to the personal obligations, responsibilities and sacrifices of parenthood. Accepting and living with these sacrifices defines motherhood and fatherhood.

It is likely that mature adolescents and dependent adults with adequate financial and educational resources will terminate their pregnancies or make adoption plans as Laura did:

It was a warm and sunny day in May that changed my life forever. The words "you're pregnant" ran through my head incessantly. How could this be? I was a 23-year-old college student who was getting ready to graduate in one month. As soon as I stopped feeling sorry for myself, my attention and energy turned to my unborn child, who was due in five months.

For me, adoption was the only real option. As much as I hated to admit it, I was not ready, or able to give my precious child the life he deserves. I wanted him to have a mother and a father, and all of the things that go along with being a real "family." I was not able to give him those things at that time.

So, I contacted several adoption agencies and chose the one that I was most comfortable with. My social worker was my rock, the one who helped me get through it all. She worked tirelessly to find the perfect parents for my baby. She was there for me before, during, and after the birth, doing all she could to make me feel comfortable, happy and loved.

My son's parents and I have a semi-open adoption, and I love seeing our son grow up through pictures and updates. I thank God every day for my son's adoptive parents. They are the most wonderful people I have ever met. I am so grateful for their generosity in allowing me to see my baby grow up. We have developed a very special relationship: one that I hope will last for a long time.

For me, adoption was definitely the best option. There are still tough days emotionally, but you must believe in your heart that you are doing the right thing for your child. And I know that my child will grow up knowing that his birthmother loves him very much and only wanted what was best for him.

Ironically, the mothers who would benefit most from making an adoption plan are the least likely to do so. They are the immature, emotionally wounded and vulnerable adolescents and dependent adults. They are dominated by fantasies and short-term urges that undermine thoughtful decision making. When these urges are accompanied by uncertainty and misconceptions about adoption, girls prefer to raise their babies, usually with the help of their relatives. For all of these reasons, Parenthood Planning Counseling for each pregnant adolescent helps to ensure that decision making meets the interests of everyone involved.

The Decision-Making Process: Parenthood Planning Counseling

In order to seriously consider whether or not to enter parenthood, a girl needs help choosing the most advantageous course. She needs to understand that her baby is not her possession and is a human being with a separate life. She needs help envisioning her future and the future of her baby. Then she can distinguish her self-interests from her baby's interests. She can see that parenthood would deprive her and her baby of vital opportunities. She can see that her parental responsibility can be fulfilled by ensuring that her baby has a family that can provide a fulfilling life.

Choosing not to enter parenthood and to make an adoption plan allows young people to develop as responsible, caring individuals. They realize they aren't ready to enter parenthood. They know they can compensate for past mistakes by not making another. They can act in the best interests of their babies, the innocent parties. They mature by planning ahead and making painful decisions. They gain satisfaction from mastering a confusing emotional crisis. They heal painful feelings by creating a better future for themselves and their babies. Sixteen-year-old Stephanie chose to make an adoption plan:

> I'm not a selfish person....A selfish person would have wanted
> to tough it out with her child and end up on welfare....The
> only thing I could give my child is love. I couldn't give her all
> that she needs. A mother who really loves her baby puts her up
> for adoption. I'm not going on welfare just to raise my child.

The sacrifice and altruism involved in adoption enables genetic mothers to see themselves as mature persons whose decisions serve their own and their babies' interests.

What Should We Do?

It is possible to mandate counseling through Parenthood Planning Teams since the newborns of minor and dependent adult parents do not have legal and physical custodians. Such a team can be activated by family planning and prenatal services that have access to pregnant adolescents and dependent adults. A mandated reporting process can be triggered as soon as an adolescent or dependent adult learns of her pregnancy and decides to continue to childbirth.

The first professional who becomes aware of a dependent person's decision to continue a pregnancy would contact the child welfare system. A Parenthood Planning Team would be formed and activate a parenthood certification process based on the Parenthood Pledge described in the next chapter. Federal law already requires in-hospital paternity acknowledgment programs to establish a baby's paternity at birth. A Parenthood Planning Team would begin this process during pregnancy through Parenthood Planning Counseling.

Chapter Fourteen

The Parenthood Pledge as the
Prerequisite for Parental Rights

*Parenthood remains the greatest single preserve
of the amateur.*

ALVIN TOFFLER, FUTURIST

Few politicians want to tackle controversial issues like poverty, race, childrearing, family structure and individual rights. Unfortunately, ensuring
that newborn babies have competent parents raises all of these issues and
seems hopeless. As a result, even though we know incompetent parents
harm their babies, families and society, we act as if there is nothing we can
do until the children are damaged. Meanwhile, we support all involved at
great cost with public and private funds.

We fail to protect newborn babies because of deeply held beliefs that
go beyond juvenile ageism. The most important is our instinctive response
to childbirth. Newborn babies belong to their mothers and fathers even if
the parents are minors or developmentally disabled. The idea of separating
babies from their families is abhorrent.

We also believe that being a parent will bring out the best in anyone. Certainly many adolescent parents have successfully raised their children and become productive citizens. Some have even become leaders and

celebrities. We want to believe everyone can succeed through hard work and effort. We specifically hope parenthood will give meaning and purpose in life to anyone.

Another deeply held belief involves accepting the consequences of our actions. The honorable response to childbirth under any circumstances might be marriage or at least for the unmarried mother and father to raise the baby. To this end, many families step forward to help their adolescent parents or to raise their grandchildren themselves.

What's more, our charitable impulses drive us to help the less fortunate. We feel obliged to minimize adversity for vulnerable parents and to improve their babies' lives through publicly funded grants, parenting education and childcare so that adolescent parents can attend school. Finally, we may not trust public or private agencies to determine whether or not a parent is competent.

Supporting vulnerable parents therefore seems to be the most practical response, but none of these impulses change the following facts:

- *People of any age who require custodians or guardians are unable to be responsible for their own lives.*

- *Adolescents are not adults and require legal and physical custodians, usually their parents.*

- *The first weeks, months and years of life are critical in child development. Babies don't benefit from waiting for adolescent parents to mature.*

PREVENTION IS KEY

We need to remind ourselves why preventing teen pregnancy is so important. Adolescent parenthood is generally regarded an undesirable lifestyle. It's an irony that while the American Humane Society restricts animal adoptions to adults we accord parental rights to minors. We assume they are capable of entering parenthood with support.

Still as a society, we actively try to prevent undesirable lifestyles. We devote public resources to preventing domestic violence, child neglect and abuse, drug abuse, alcoholism, smoking, obesity, sexually transmitted diseases and adolescent pregnancy. When individuals persist in such behaviors despite interventions, we take one of two courses:

- When harm involves only the individual, we care for them. For example, our health care systems help both smokers and nonsmokers.

- When behavior harms others, as with sexually transmitted diseases, public health and law enforcement systems intervene. Adolescent parenthood has repercussions far beyond the parents. Its short- and long-term effects harm their babies, their families and our society.

Nevertheless, we automatically shift from teen pregnancy prevention to childrearing support of adolescent parents based on our perceived lack of alternatives and our desire to minimize harm to the baby. Focusing only on the baby ignores the interests of the adolescent. Focusing only on the adolescent ignores the interests of the baby. In both situations, the interests of the family and society are ignored.

Instead of these fragmented responses, the birth of babies to adolescents should evoke full consideration first of the interests of the babies, then of the adolescents, then of their relatives and ultimately of society. We haven't carefully thought through these issues. As a result, our responses are reactive rather than proactive.

Child psychiatrist Paul Trad noted that adolescent childbirth is a high-risk crisis that warrants sensitive, realistic intervention. We need a paradigm that protects everyone's interests. That paradigm will recognize the fact that adolescent childbirth is an even greater public health crisis than adolescent pregnancy. This paradigm also can be applied to childbirth by adults with legal guardians and by adults courts have found to be unfit parents.

Soft Paternalism (Parentalism)

To counter advocates who regard intrusion on a parent's privacy as objectionable paternalism, the idea of *soft paternalism* or *parentalism* has been advanced. Rebecca Maynard, professor of education and social policy at the

University of Pennsylvania, suggests soft paternalism as an appropriate way to help people prone to self-defeating behaviors. Missouri, for example, makes it illegal for persons identified as compulsive gamblers to enter casinos.

Maynard suggests that soft paternalism be applied to adolescent pregnancy and childbirth. Speed limits and traffic lights are everyday examples of public interventions that protect us from the acts of others as well as our own impulses. We expect protection from unethical businesses and professionals. Only by having consequences for undesirable actions can we maintain an open society.

But the word paternalism, even soft paternalism, has a sexist flavor. It evokes images of governmental control of private lives and abuse of the disadvantaged. These concerns are valid when a public policy has unintended consequences that override its benefits. Policies based on value judgments, such as "all cohabiting couples should be married," are examples. This argument doesn't apply to policies based on scientific evidence where benefits unmistakably outweigh potential adverse effects.

Such is the case with adolescent and dependent adult childbirth that has demonstrated undesirable consequences. A less controversial term would convey the need to protect individuals through regulations that serve their interests. I suggest the term *parentalism*. It conveys the need for a society to protect and nurture its members. Our governments already apply parentalism in their *in loco parentis* role under the *parens patriae* doctrine that supports parental authority and limits the privileges of adolescents who might make harmful life-altering decisions.

SETTING STANDARDS FOR PARENTHOOD

The public currently supports parenthood through tax benefits, public education and public assistance. To justify this support, we need greater accountability for parents. We should link the public benefits of parenthood to an individual's capacity to fulfill parenthood's responsibilities. The ability to conceive and give birth says nothing about a parent's competence. We need to evaluate a parent's competence by setting minimum standards for parenthood based on our cultural expectations.

We already have precedents for establishing legal spousal relationships in the marriage license application. Most states have three requirements for a legal marital relationship.

1) *Affidavit*: A declaration under oath that the information provided is true and that no legal impediment exists to entering marriage. The affidavit contains:

- Proof of age and residence eligibility;

- Information about previous marriages;

- Social Security number; and

- That the marriage is not between genetic relatives.

2) *License*: Authorizes the marriage ceremony after a waiting period.
3) *Certificate of Marriage*: Executed by a legally authorized official.

Marriage has been considered to be a precursor to parenthood. The importance of the parent-child relationship to our society in the absence of marriage makes it even more imperative to sett minimum standards for the legal relationship between parent and child as marriage does for spouses. The incompetence of millions of contemporary parents makes this a critical issue. Legislated standards are needed to set forth integrative cultural values that further the common good through committed relationships between parents and children.

Setting standards for parenthood can be done on two legal grounds: a social power to maintain stability and order in our society and a *parens patriae* power to protect the welfare of those unable to act in their own best interests.

James Dwyer, professor of law at William and Mary University, proposes that certain high-risk parents be required to certify that they meet minimum standards before becoming the legal and physical custodians of their children. Wisconsin Cares, Inc., a family advocacy organization, proposes that these standards stem from the principle that *a person who requires a legal and physical custodian or guardian or who has been found to be a legally unfit parent cannot be the legal and physical custodian of a newborn baby.*

Dwyer points out that newborn babies have a moral right as well as a Constitutional right under the Due Process Clause of the Fourteenth Amendment that prevents the state from placing newborn babies in a legal relationship with birth parents who are known to be unfit. This would commonly mean minor parents because they require legal and physical custodians themselves. Less commonly, it would include the developmentally disabled or mentally ill with legal guardians, persons incarcerated for violent crimes and individuals already adjudicated to be unfit parents.

Legal standards for competence and for being a custodian or guardian of other persons vary by jurisdiction. Generally they embody the ability to understand relevant information and consequences of behavior, to make choices through mature reasoning and to communicate these choices. The criteria for obtaining a marriage license address these capacities. Mental health professionals use additional tools to assess the competence of mentally ill and developmentally disabled parents for courts.

DETERMINING ELIGIBILITY FOR PARENTHOOD

If we accept the premise that parenthood is a vital career that involves the legal and physical custody of a child with inherent duties, how do we determine who is eligible for parenthood?

One way is through setting an age at which the presumption can be made that a person is able to assume to these responsibilities. This has the advantage of simplicity and the disadvantage of not taking into account individual circumstances. The second is to establish a licensing procedure through which one can demonstrate the capacities to assume the duties of parenthood. This has the advantage of accommodating individual circumstances and the disadvantage of devising a licensing process. In recent decades Hugh LaFollette, Michael McFall, Mark Vopat, Peg Tittle and I are among those who have contributed to a movement to institute a parent licensing process like that involved in obtaining a license to drive a motor vehicle, a much less demanding social responsibility.

Because the licensing parents movement has not resulted in concrete action, Wisconsin Cares, Inc., proposes a simple procedure for formally awarding parental rights through the Parenthood Pledge in a birth certificate application with eligibility to make the Pledge determined simply by the fact that a conceiving person is not under the custody or guardianship of another person or the state. When a person is not eligible to make the Pledge, the status of the newborn baby would be determined through Parenthood Planning Counseling. There are two circumstances under which a person would not meet this standard. The first is being a legal minor. The second is being an adult who a court has determined to need a guardian or who a court has determined unfit to be a parent.

In awarding social privileges, an age is necessary in order to provide a guideline for statutes. For this reason, there are a series of ages at which privileges are awarded for the ability to drive a motor vehicle, enter contracts, vote, marry, enter the military service and generally achieve adulthood. The "age of majority" is construed to mean the age at which one is "emancipated from infancy" and enters adulthood. In the United States majority status is attained at the age of 18 except for Alabama where it is 20 and for Mississippi and Puerto Rico where it is 21. The National Minimum Drinking Age Act of 1984 withholds revenues from states that allow the purchase of alcohol by anyone under the age of 21. Some privileges, such as driving a motor vehicle, require demonstration of the ability to handle the privilege in addition to age eligibility.

Under ideal circumstances from the point of view of a prospective parent and unborn child, parenthood should follow completion of the adolescent stage of development. The physical and psychological development involved in adolescence extends from puberty to adulthood and has three stages: *early* adolescence (ages eleven through fourteen); *middle* adolescence (ages fifteen through seventeen); and *late* adolescence (ages eighteen to twenty-one). In addition to physiological growth, key intellectual, psychological and social developmental tasks are accomplished these years. The fundamental purpose of these tasks is to form one's own identity and to prepare for adulthood. Following this definition of adulthood and the licensing of motor vehicle drivers, the age of eligibility for parenthood would be 21, and a demonstration of the ability to handle the privilege would be required.

There is another reason to exclude 18, 19 and 20-year-old adolescents from eligibility for parenthood. They are likely to be living alone or with transient males and are more prone to neglect and abuse their children than school age adolescents who are likely to be living with their parents.

Whatever age is selected, there is the need to specify a reasonable time, such as six-months before that date so that the imminence of eligibility for parenthood is taken into account. This could be 17½ if the eligibility age is 18.

All of this merits careful consideration and discussion. The complicated issues involved really boil down to ensuring that newborn babies have competent parents who can nurture them with adequate shelter, food, clothing, health care and education.

From the practical point of view at this time, the most feasible approach may well be to begin with the simple requirement that a person meet a state's age of majority. This is a requirement now for minor parents who must have an adult or institutional payee in order to receive Temporary Assistance for Needy Families benefits. This approach would open the door to focusing attention on the issues involved and to further consideration of the next step to a parent licensing process that could enable distinguishing between 18 through 20-year-old adolescents who are capable of entering parenthood from those who are not.

THE CERTIFICATION OF PARENTHOOD

A birth certificate is a vital record like a marriage certificate. Issued shortly after birth, it is generated when the mother's health care provider files the required forms with a state agency. It contains detailed information about the birth, baby, parents and family. It also could confirm that the parents are committed to parenthood and meet minimum standards for legal and physical custodianship of the newborn baby.

The birth certificate process could be modified to include a paragraph setting forth the minimum standards for parenthood used by family courts, which are basically to:

- Ensure that a child receives nurturance and life's material necessities.

- Make prudent decisions concerning the child's welfare and wellbeing.

- Arrange for and authorize health care.

- Advocate the child's interests.

The following Parenthood Pledge could be signed by all mothers and fathers:

> I *understand and accept the responsibilities of parenthood for* _____ *and will carry them out to the best of my ability.*

Following Dwyer's reasoning high-risk parents could be identified as soon as possible before childbirth. By drawing upon the health, child welfare, correctional and birth registration systems, the birth certificate application process could become a meaningful step toward ensuring a newborn's actual wellbeing. This process could be initiated at one of three points. In order of desirability, they are:

1) When a pregnancy is identified;
2) When prenatal care begins; and
3) On admission to a hospital or birthing center.

At the first point of contact when a pregnancy is identified, professionals could note the ages of all mothers and check public databases for relevant correctional records. A qualified social worker could access child protective services data. If the pregnancy is terminated, the pregnancy will be counted in state and national health statistics. Indeed, some states already require reporting for pregnancy terminations and fetal deaths.

The birth certificate could be modified so that it becomes a certificate of parenthood that explicitly conveys legal and physical custodianship. Because the babies of minor parents do not have legal and physical custodians, a statutory requirement could be created or interpreted so that babies born to mothers under a certain age, such as 17½, are assigned legal and physical custodians who are either willing and able relatives or adoptive parents through a voluntary or involuntary adoption plan.

The Certification Process

In the proposed certification process, when a pregnancy is identified and the decision is made to continue to childbirth, those eligible for automatic certification would be informed about making a Parenthood Pledge. Those ineligible for automatic certification would be contacted by a child welfare worker. A Parenthood Planning Team would be formed and counsel them and their families.

For the dependent parent, counseling would include 1) identifying adults qualified to assume legal and physical custodianship of the newborn baby or 2) making an adoption plan. The team would help adults interested in custodianship determine if they are capable of assuming the following custodianship responsibilities:

1) continue to provide legal and physical custodianship of the dependent mother or father;
2) provide childrearing resources, including shelter, clothing and food for the
3) mother or father and baby; and
4) advocate for the parent and the baby, including the ability to provide health care.

If they are willing and able to do so they would be the legal and physical custodians recorded on the birth certificate by co-signing the Parenthood Pledge.

When no adult family member is willing and able to assume legal and physical custodianship of the newborn child, a Child in Need of Protection Services petition would be filed. A court would appoint a guardian *ad litem* to the Parenthood Planning Team. The guardian *ad litem* would represent the unborn baby, seek termination of parental rights and make an adoption plan. The birth certificate would record a state or private agency as the legal and physical custodian until the adoption is finalized.

If an adolescent or dependent adult gives birth without prenatal care, the hospital now can immediately refer the case to child welfare services. The lack of prenatal care itself constitutes medical neglect that requires investigation and is grounds for automatic termination of parental rights followed by adoption. The state is recorded as the legal and physical custodian until an individual is appointed as custodian or the adoption is finalized.

Model for a Parenthood Certification Process	
Automatic Certification Adults Procedure Sign Parenthood Pledge with birth registration application.	Certification of Co-signer by Application 1) Minors with or without parents (legal and physical Custodians) 2) Adults with guardians 3) Adults adjudicated as unfit parents 4) Adults current incarcerated Procedure 1) Parenthood Planning Team is formed to provide Parenthood Planning Counseling at the time pregnancy is diagnosed. 2) Formulation of a voluntary adoption plan is considered. 3) Qualified relative is co-signer of the Parenthood Pledge and becomes the temporary or permanent legal and physical custodian of the newborn baby. 4) If there is no relative qualified to be a legal and physical custodian, a guardian ad litem is appointed to institute an involuntary termination of parental rights with an adoption plan at birth.

This model would be implemented by identifying dependent mothers and fathers at the earliest possible time. The birth registration process would be expanded to include certification that a parent has made a commitment to carry out the responsibilities of parenthood. This would include:

1) Automatic certification of parenthood for mothers and fathers who are adults and sign the Parenthood Pledge.
2) A certification application and review process when a mother or father is:
   a) a legal minor under 17 ½ at due date;
   b) developmentally disabled or mentally ill adult with a guardian;

c) adjudicated as an unfit parent because of child neglect or abuse; or

d) currently incarcerated.

Objections to a Certification Process

This proposal will face resistance because it appears to add new burdens to legal and social service systems already strained by child neglect and abuse. It invokes images of government restrictions on individual liberties, the invasion of family privacy and the stigmatization of dependent parents. Some adults might feel insulted by being required to sign the Parenthood Pledge even though they would not feel that way about any other licensing or contract process. Allegations of "genocide" of minorities and punishing people living in poverty also can be expected. It might even appear to presume guilt unless innocence is proved for those believe that the role of government is limited to intervening after harms have occurred. It might place health care professionals in the position of reporting pregnancies and conflict with their ethical codes.

None of these objections are substantive or valid. Establishing eligibility to make the Parenthood Pledge is not:

1) Eugenics: It does not affect conception except as it causes people to think more seriously about conceiving and raising a child.

2) Against the human right to procreate: The survival of the species mandates the right of every human being to procreate, but the survival of the species also depends upon the ability of a parent to fulfill the duty to competently raise a child that is inherent in that right.

3) Racist: Weighting toward minority groups is coincidental, not targeted. Most minority parents are competent parents.

4) Discrimination against the poor: Weighting toward the disadvantaged is coincidental. Many parents living in poverty are competent parents.

5) Elitist: Wealthy parents can be incompetent.

6) <u>An unconstitutional invasion of the privacy of the family</u>: The Parenthood Pledge would explicitly award now implicit parental rights and call attention to their accompanying responsibilities. States now have the power to set and regulate family policies as expressed in child abuse and neglect, child custody and termination of parental rights statutes.

7) <u>An intrusion on individual liberty</u>: States have the responsibility to regulate individual actions that can potentially harm other persons through establishing qualifications and licensing, such as through licensing motor vehicle drivers, trades and professions. Parents are not at liberty to harm their children.

8) <u>Impractical</u>: The Parenthood Pledge can be easily incorporated in the birth registration application and become a certification of parenthood in the birth certificate.

9) <u>Costly</u>: The volume of Parenthood Planning Counseling would increase the number of professionals needed to implement it. However, the immediate savings in health care costs and the short- and long-term savings in educational, mental health, social services and correctional costs would offset those comparatively infinitesimal costs.

Certifying a person's qualification for parenthood would demonstrate that our society places a high value on ensuring that all children have competent parents. It would signal that we recognize parenthood as a valued career for which we have established minimum standards.

A FEASIBLE PLAN

Since adolescents gradually assume adult responsibilities, we set ages for awarding each responsibility. Because of the impact adolescent childbirth has on our society and because the average age of menarche is twelve, we must establish an age at which parenthood can be entered and legal and physical custodianship of a newborn baby can be assumed. This is particularly important because adolescent parenthood raises a baby's risk of prematurity, morbidity, developmental problems, neglect and abuse. The most sensible and realistic approach is to recognize dependent-parent childbirth as the serious public health crisis that it is.

In our culture, dependent parenthood is undesirable for parents and babies. In spite of this, we provide financial, educational and group home support for adolescent mothers and their babies who too often are harmed despite the support.

The most striking aspect of adolescent and dependent adult childbirth is that the newborn baby doesn't have a legal and physical custodian.

Without creating a new bureaucracy, we can organize Parenthood Planning Teams from family planning, prenatal care, child welfare, home visitation and legal programs that already exist. We can follow the model of crisis-intervention teams that address other health and child welfare matters. Parenthood Planning Teams can guide adolescents and dependent adults and their families to make sound decisions as is already required for federal Adolescent Family Life Demonstration Projects.

The goal is to act *before* birth. When a dependent parent's baby is born, three reasonable outcomes exist:

1) Relatives continue custodianship of the dependent parent and assume temporary or permanent custodianship of the newborn baby;

2) The dependent parents and their families make a voluntary adoption plan; or

3) A Parenthood Planning Team makes an involuntary adoption plan for the baby when relatives are unwilling and/or unable to assume custodianship of the dependent mother and her baby. Adoption offers the most practical and available access to competent parents for babies who do not have competent parents.

Most importantly, the Parenthood Pledge and Parenthood Certification would be concrete symbols of our society's devotion to our children and to our own future prosperity. In addition to the long-term result of providing an opportunity for success in life for newborn babies, it would have the short-term effect of removing the status, financial and other supportive benefits that provide incentives for dependent persons to give birth and to become parents.

Chapter Fifteen

Barriers to Change and Hope for the Future

When reality is unpleasant, illusions offer an attractive escape route. In difficult times unscrupulous manipulators enjoy a competitive advantage over those who seek to confront reality.

GEORGE SOROS
PHILANTHROPIST

The most important barriers to constructive social change are 1) "totalism"; 2) reactions to instability and human differences; 3) the financial benefits of status-quo inefficiency; 4) weak social capital; 5) the failure of families and schools to develop the analytic and collaborative skills individuals need for teamwork; and 6) mistrust of government institutions.

TOTALISM

The greatest barrier to constructive social change is what psychohistorian Robert Jay Lifton called *totalism.* This occurs when political or religious systems seek to stamp out independent thought. Totalism is particularly attractive when systems are on the edge of chaos. When we are confronted by something so big it requires us to change the way we think and the way we see the world, denial is a natural response. Denial keeps our minds from becoming overloaded.

An example of totalism is the polarization of political parties. At a time when the public is open to changes, both political parties have become more rigid by representing special interest groups that trump the common good by encouraging opposition to, rather than interaction with, people with different ideas. This promotes single-mindedness and resistance to problem solving, which involves collaboration and teamwork.

INSTABILITY AND HUMAN DIFFERENCES

Psychiatrist and systems analyst Denis Donovan points out that most Americans can't stand instability. Just when a system, such as education, mental health, health care or human services, is loosening up enough to reorganize itself, it destabilizes. We jump in to stabilize the system and prevent adaptive reorganization. When that system fails to reorganize, it then is seen as seriously flawed and becomes more unstable.

At the level of individual differences, Princeton social psychologist Susan Fiske says that two emotions lie at the heart of a vast number of interpersonal, societal and international tensions: envy and scorn. Our human tendency is to compare ourselves to others and to compare our group to other groups. We envy people who are higher in competence and/or power. We scorn people who are lower in competence and/or power either by pitying or being disgusted with them.

In groups, these emotions spawn stereotypes that lead to prejudice and discrimination...especially during stressful times. Globally, the United States is widely perceived as powerful and thus can face envy and distrust from other parts of the world. Within the United States, educated people can be scorned as impractical or out of touch. Uneducated persons can be seen as lacking intelligence.

Gender differences are particularly relevant when it comes to childbirth and childrearing. Women can see men as being biased and vice versa. Homemaking roles are especially associated with male and female stereotypes. The fact that males simply conceive and females conceive and bear children has powerful effects on the way that people perceive motherhood and fatherhood. This spills over into negative reactions of females to proposals made by males and vice versa.

THE FINANCIAL BENEFITS OF INEFFICIENCY

In 1961 President Dwight Eisenhower warned about the military-industrial complex that spawned unnecessary projects and costs. In 1965, Secretary of Defense Robert McNamara highlighted how the efficiency of a system, in this case the military forces, was less important than expansion of private-sector defense expenditures. A similar case can be made for service industries that depend upon the products of incompetent parents.

Today our nation is shining a bright light on the economics of the conflict between cutting public costs and creating and saving jobs. For example, most of the money related to the "get tough on crime" movement is spent on imprisonment which creates jobs. This means cutting funds for prevention, treatment, education and resources that would keep over half the prisoners with mental illnesses and drug problems out of prison in the first place. Efforts are made to keep prisons open even when they no longer are needed to maintain local jobs and businesses. Job security trumps cutting incarceration costs. A hidden agenda of get-tough policies can even be to imprison as many people as possible to support local economies and to privatize public prisons.

What's more the health care, mental health and human services systems are highly fragmented. This leads to redundancy, inefficiency and reduced efficacy. Primary care and mental health clinicians have been locked into traditions that separate them. About 65% of Americans are overweight or obese and most are resistant to weight loss. The excess weight costs our nation an estimated $93 billion in medical bills every year. If these systems functioned more efficiently, overall costs would be reduced significantly. But this also means that anyone who would lose revenue has an incentive to oppose reforming these systems.

Today, psychiatry and psychology aren't calling for social policies and neighborhood interventions that shield children from stressors that weaken families and limit the growth, health, learning and wellbeing of entire populations. Instead the focus is on brain development, the early diagnosis of problems and medications.

Finally, collaboration inside bureaucracies is a concept more often lauded than enacted. Rigid funding pathways (silos), tradition and territoriality stand in the way. Even communities with a long history of activism struggle with getting groups that can learn from each other to plan projects for their mutual benefit. At the same time, in her book, *Quiet: The Power of Introverts in a World That Can't Stop Talking*, Susan Cain points out that efforts to force collaboration through offices without walls, structured groupthink and confusing social skills with the ability to work in teams can backfire when constant interruptions kill creativity.

Here is a typical example of collaborative failure at the state level. In April, 2000, Wisconsin Governor Tommy Thompson created the Governor's Blue-Ribbon Commission on State-Local Partnerships for the Twenty-First Century. He charged it with conducting a "mini-constitutional convention" to rethink what Wisconsin government does and how it can perform better with less money. In January of 2001 the Commission laid out a bold strategy that emphasized innovative partnerships among Wisconsin's state and local governments. The strategy aimed to improve the quality of life for all state citizens and deliver better value for taxpayers' dollars. It would have reduced tension in the political system and made Wisconsin's state and local governments genuine partners instead of adversaries. Over the following decade, few of its proposals saw the light of day.

WEAK SOCIAL CAPITAL

Weakened social capital is seen in things that have vanished almost unnoticed from our society…neighborhood parties and get-togethers with friends, the unconditional kindness of strangers and a shared pursuit of the public good rather than the solitary quest for private goods.

Harvard Professor of Public Policy Robert Putnam noted in *Bowling Alone* that the changing character of work and the closely related flow of women into the workforce were among the most far-reaching upheavals of the Twentieth Century. This workplace transformation was comparable to the metamorphosis of America from a nation of farms to one of factories and offices. Public and private American institutions and norms as well as workplace practices have only begun to adapt to the shift of mothers from homes to workplaces. This workplace revolution contributed to the decline in face-to-face social connectedness and civic involvement now aggravated by communication through social media. At the same time the social media do offer the potential for changing perceptions and stimulating constructive actions.

LACK OF ANALYTIC AND COLLABORATIVE SKILLS

David Boulton, learning technologist and creator of *Children of the Code,* asks how families, schools and social support systems might differ if their central organizing principle was driven by how well children learn to solve problems rather than how well they learn outdated, adult-centric lessons.

Even intelligent and well-educated people accept information from an apparently authoritative source rather than thinking analytically. If a statement begins, "Neuroscience tells us that" then finishes with nonsense, a significant percentage will simply accept it. If the same assertion is made without reference to neuroscience, they recognize that the statement makes no sense. Our perceptions of reality are dependent upon the beliefs we hold. This is belief-dependent "reality."

At a more personal level, Boulton points out that most children who struggle with learning to read English believe something is wrong with themselves...something to be ashamed of. Unintentionally but pervasively parents, schools and society contribute to this myth. Children don't think that the trouble might be normal differences in their genes and brains the same way people can be tall or short. They don't suspect that their parents, siblings and caregivers might not have engaged them enough in conversation before they started school. They don't wonder if their teachers didn't teach them well. They don't know that the complicated English language presents an unnatural processing challenge. They blame themselves. They feel ashamed of themselves...ashamed of their minds. Statements like "I'm dumb," "I'm stupid" and "I'm not good in school" reflect their shame.

Walking, talking, reading, writing, math, science, art, politics, philosophy, physical health, emotional wellbeing, financial security, upward mobility, family harmony, social responsibility and spiritual attunement... there isn't any human activity that is not enhanced and constrained by learning. Learning how to think critically and to solve problems is as relevant to personal, corporate, national and world problem solving as it is

to a parent's love, achieving an individual's potential and the quest for scientific, artistic, philosophical and spiritual truths. The most practical and
profound response to ambiguities in school, at home, on the job and in
society is to learn how to invent and reinvent…the foundation of collaboration and teamwork.

Today's young people generally have had more structure than any other generation in American history. They are supervised, coached and tu-
tored to prepare them for success in school. Students are encouraged to
follow personal passions and dreams to align themselves with American
individualism.

Most contemporary young adults will not get married, buy a house and
have children in the sequence followed by previous generations. Most will
spend a decade searching for their role in our society. Many are unprepared
for an uncertain, open world in which success is determined by their useful-
ness to others.

In order to succeed, they will discover that the social purpose of their
life is not to find themselves by pursuing their passions. Instead, it is to
lose themselves in serving others. The flourishing young adult commits
to a spouse and a community. Genuine success in life is not achieved from
satisfying our inner world desires but from our significance to others in our
outer world.

MISTRUST OF GOVERNMENT INSTITUTIONS

There are good reasons for concern about government overreaching in
family and juvenile behavioral matters. Examples range from the notori-
ous misuse and failures of foster care to overreaction to the 2012 Newton,
Connecticut, school shooting though "zero tolerance" of such behavior as
pointing a finger and pretending to shoot a classmate.

As this book has demonstrated, the failure of government institutions
to intervene in family lives in a timely and appropriate manner is a far
greater concern than governmental overreaching. Still no public or private
system operates perfectly. For this reason involuntary actions arising from
Parenthood Planning Counseling and the Parenthood Pledge are designed
to include the checks and balances of the courts, such as by appointing a

guardian *ad litem* for the unborn child when an involuntary adoption is planned at birth.

THE GOOD NEWS

In *The Evolution of Virtue, Altruism, and Shame*, Christopher Boehm presents evidence for the evolution of the human capacity for bonding, collaboration and altruism. As collaboration was necessary for efficient hunting, natural selection favored individuals who were better at inhibiting their own anti-social tendencies, either through fear of punishment or through absorbing and identifying with their group's rules. Competition, territoriality and tribalism rooted in our reptilian brains served humans well in less complicated worlds but so did cooperation and the ability to trust and bond rooted in our forebrains. While competition is a key driver in human evolution and human affairs, collaboration and teamwork are equally if not more important.

In her book *Building a Win-Win World*, economist Hazel Henderson offers hope for the future global economy. She demonstrates how the present global economy is unsustainable because of its negative effects on employees, families, communities and the ecosystem. She sees a shift taking place from a value-system based on competition, conflict and what she calls "economism" (an approach that puts economics at the center of public policy and reduces individual and public choices to matters of self-interest and rationality) toward a value-system based on interdependence, sustainability and cooperation. In her view, a "quality-of-life" language is emerging that opens the way for new approaches to our national and global problems. There is "slow-motion good news" going on, she says, as the old ways of doing things are challenged by "global citizens," grassroots organizations and enlightened businesses around the world.

HUMAN NATURAL CAPITAL

Our focus on enhancing our *nonhuman natural capital* (the physical environment) can be complemented by a focus on our *human natural capital* (our young citizens). John McNight, professor of education and social policy at Northwestern University, notes that our roles as citizens have been subordinated to our roles as clients and consumers. Many of us have become too impotent to be called real citizens and too disconnected to be effective members of a community.

Still there is a growing recognition that we have lost a shared national purpose. We want to improve our own lives and our nation. We find agreement about integrity, fairness, altruism, responsibility, respect and valor in all our ethnic subcultures. It's time for our governments and the marketplace to create new forms of collaboration that enhance human natural capital. Over 1,200 companies have signed the ten principles of Global Corporate Citizenship of the Global Compact launched by the United Nations in 2000. The compact covers human rights, workplace safety, justice, anti-corruption measures and environmental sustainability.

Democracy is more than a system of government. It enables people to act together in the pursuit of common goals and aspirations. In her book *Collective Visioning: How Groups Can Work Together for a Just and Sustainable Future*, community organizer Linda Stout describes how people can rally others to work toward common goals. Democracy depends upon its human ecosystem: civil alliances, social norms and deliberative practices with a self-organizing rather than an institutional quality.

Improving public policy is not always a matter of making it more responsive to the public will. It also means addressing social and political inequalities. When conflicts and disagreements arise, deliberation allows groups to arrive at a collective assessment that is more than the sum of individual opinions and preferences. The electronic social media allow us to come together more easily to create and sustain community and political movements. The health of a community, state or nation can be measured by its social capital its informal networks of reciprocity, trust and mutual assistance.

The social networking organization Zocalo Public Square joined with Arizona State University and the New America Foundation to launch the non-partisan Center for Social Cohesion. The Center will study the forces that shape our sense of social unity. Its mission is to bring people together to understand our challenges today so we can more realistically address them tomorrow.

SHIFT FROM AND INDIVIDUAL TO A FAMILY FOCUS

The natural tendency is to think of persons as individuals. This is appropriate under many circumstances but not when issues affect the lives of these individuals. Mothers and fathers of minors have children and youth who depend upon them. Children and youth likewise have parents who are affected by their actions. Even a focus on children and families implies that children are freestanding individuals apart from their families. This is why "child-saver" organizations have failed. They need to be family-focused organizations in order to fulfill their missions.

As an example of an effort to shift from an individual to a family focus and provide a forum for Collaborative Systems of Care at the state level in Wisconsin, Wisconsin Cares, Inc., has proposed a Family Policy Integration Board to coordinate nine government agencies that impact families. This board would relate to a collaborative structure in each county, tribe or service area with an operational agreement created by an executive committee of public and private stakeholders. Such structures now exist in over 55 counties and tribes in Wisconsin.

The existing state Child Abuse and Neglect Prevention Board would be transformed into a Family Policy Integration Board that would relate to local collaboratives; facilitate collaboration and integration between agencies; evaluate the impact of legislation on families; and recommend legislative initiatives. The Board would avoid creating additional costs by drawing upon and realigning personnel from existing agencies. It would view policies from the standpoint of *families* rather than *children and families.* This means that children would not be considered free-standing individuals who are not parts of families. When a parent is not willing or able to fulfill the best interests of a child, the focus would be on helping the parent do so or on replacing the parent with a competent adoptive parent rather than placing the child in indefinite foster care without such a plan. The principle is that a child is incomplete without a competent parent.

Innovative Schools

The Knowledge Is Power Program (KIPP) is a network of charter schools that serve over 26,000 students. It offers a rigorous college-preparatory curriculum to students who would otherwise be relegated to substandard neighborhood schools. Staff visit families so parents can sign and fulfill contracts in which they promise to help with homework, read to their kids nightly and volunteer at school. Learning is a collaborative family-school process.

Since 1907 when Maria Montessori launched her first school in Rome, her enduring philosophy has revolved around a simple principle: curiosity drives kids to learn. Today an estimated 4,000 Montessori schools operate in the United States. Clark Montessori Junior & Senior High School in Cincinnati, Ohio, is the first public junior high and high school to encourage children to follow their interests in problem solving. Collaboration is key. Each year the 600 or so students sign a contract pledging to help build the school community as well as the community outside school. Students are required to perform 200 hours of community service in order to graduate.

Imagine what it would be like if each person attaining the age of legal majority pledged to abide by our nation's cultural values embedded in our laws as is required of naturalized citizens. Skeptics would say it would make no difference but it would make a greater impression on youth than the occasional pledge of allegiance to our flag.

A NATIONAL PARENT ORGANIZATION

The American Association of Retired Persons is a powerful organization that lobbies for the interests of older persons. Scores of advocacy organizations for children have more or less influence over specific public policies that affect children and youth. Strikingly, there is no National Association of Parents devoted to advocate the needs of families. Parents apparently are too busy raising their children to establish and maintain a national organization.

Parents are represented now by organizations that focus on education and special needs. The National Parent Teacher Association (PTA) is the most influential. Its 2012 policy agenda advocates family engagement in schools and overall improvements in general, special and early childhood education. The PTA also is a strong advocate for increased education funding. It prioritizes the health and wellbeing of children through implementation of, and improvements in, nutrition laws. It aims to protect the rights of children and youth in the justice system.

The National Association of Parents with Children in Special Education renders support and assistance to parents whose children receive special education services inside and outside school. It was founded to provide parents with children with special needs a sense of community and a national forum for their ideas.

The *National Association for Parents of Children* with Visual Impairments enables parents to find information and resources for children who are blind or visually impaired. The National Autism Association responds to the most urgent needs of the autism community, providing real help and hope so that everyone can reach their full potential.

The National Association of Grandparents and Other Caregivers provides networking, support and education to caregivers. Generations United is a national coalition dedicated to intergenerational policy programs and issues. The Foundation for Grandparenting is a nonprofit organization that raises grandparent consciousness. It also promotes the importance of grandparenting as a role and function that creates meaning and empowerment in later life while benefiting all family members.

These organizations perform important functions for specific interest groups, but we need an umbrella National Association of Parents dedicated to promoting parenthood and family resources for all parents.

A VISION FOR THE FUTURE

The prosperity of our nation depends upon all of our children and adolescents becoming productive citizens. Our Declaration of Independence declares that all newborn babies–as our *posterity*–are entitled to an opportunity to become productive citizens. All adolescents deserve to work through the joys and discomforts of adolescence without having their growing bodies, minds and personalities burdened by pregnancy and parenthood. All parents deserve to raise their adolescents without the responsibility of rearing another generation.

There is a difference between being a parent and embracing parenthood as a career. We cannot expect dependent persons to avoid parenthood until society affirms that parenthood is a rewarding, lifelong, sacrificial calling for those who are capable of assuming its responsibilities. We betray their trust when we do not protect pregnant adolescents prior to childbirth from decisions that profoundly alter the courses of their lives.

Our society doesn't have a way of ensuring that genetic parents are competent and accountable. Legal and physical custody of a newborn is given to anyone who conceived that child regardless of that person's ability to raise a child. We don't intervene until that child has been damaged by abuse or neglect.

Most thoughtful Americans value the responsibility, integrity, opportunity and privacy embodied in competent parenthood. When all children have competent parents with adequate resources for achieving skills and generating hope for the future, our society will have overcome juvenile ageism. This vision is not pie-in-the-sky thinking. We can move forward strongly if we act upon the simple fact that minor and dependent adult parents require legal and physical custodians themselves and therefore cannot be the custodians of other persons. They are incapable of being competent parents. This will help break the cycle of intergenerational poverty.

This vision can be achieved if we value parenthood as a vital career that requires basic managerial skills and essential resources. The Parenthood Pledge as a part of the birth certificate process would make explicit our implicit social contract between parents and society. This Pledge could only be made by those who aren't under the custody or guardianship of others. This Pledge would have a profound effect on our society by affirming through small but crucial actions that newborn babies are valued by our society and are full-fledged citizens with the right to have competent parents who can give them an opportunity to succeed in life.

Because our society doesn't articulate its expectations for parents, child neglect and abuse in the United States have reached epidemic proportions and exceed rates in all other developed nations. We only intervene after children have been damaged by neglect and abuse, often ineffectively. Enormous public expenditures on treatment, rehabilitation and incarceration follow. This would change dramatically if our vision for America was that all of our children would be raised by competent parents.

APPENDIX 1

Financial Cost of an Habitual Criminal from a Single-Parent Family Receiving Public Benefits

1. Lived at home with single mother (from birth to 13 years):
TANF payments $ 61,400
social services ($2,633 x 13)   40,200

2. Lived at home with parent (ages 13 to 15 years):
arrests by police (3) $ 750
court costs (2)   5,520
detained overnight (1)   128
probation services   6,320

3. Juvenile correctional institution (ages 15 to 15 1/4 years):
arrest by police (1) $ 260
court cost (1)   2,770
detained overnight (1)   128
correctional facilities   12,690

4. Lived at home with parent (ages 15 1/4 to 17 1/4years):
probation (1 year) $ 3,160
arrest by police (1)   260
court cost (1)   2,775

5. Lived at home with parent (ages 15 1/4 to 17 1/4years):
probation (1 year) $ 3,160
arrest by police (1)   260
court cost (1)   2,775

6. Adult prison (ages 18 to 60 years; 42 years prison):
court costs (3 x $2,775) $ 8,320
arrests by police (3 x $260)   780
jail detention ($128 x 60)   7,680
adult prison ($25,500 x 40)   1,071,000

Total Juvenile Cost: $142,556
Total Adult Cost: $1,087,780

Total Direct Cost for Services: $1,230,336

Loss of Federal Income Taxes ($30,000 single person: $ 3,000 x 42): $126,000
Total Direct Cost to Government: $1,356,336

Loss to National Economy ($36,000 x 42 years): $1,512,000

Total Monetary Cost to Society for Individual: $2,868,336

APPENDIX 2

Public Expenditures Related to Struggling Families
(Largely federal funds passed through states to localities)

Wisconsin Executive Budget 2012

Calculated by Departments		Struggling Families
Department of Corrections		$1.2 billion
Department of Health Services	8.8 billion	2.8 billion
(Medicaid – 28% low income & 20% elderly 2.8 billion)		
Department of Children and Families		1.3 billion
Department of Public Instruction		.2 billion
Special Education .54 billion (Behavioral categories .2 billion)		
Department of Workforce Development 1.2 billion		1.2 billion
(Workforce development .3 billion)		
(Economic support .9 billion)		
Youth Aids		.1 billion
Office of Justice Assistance		
Juvenile delinquency		.2 billion
		Total $7 billion
		(23% of $30 billion)

Wisconsin County Budgets
(Wisconsin Taxpayers Alliance)

Total Expenditures (2010)		$5.3 billion
Law enforcement		.76 billion
Jail costs	$ .48 billion	
Juvenile & Domestic Violence	$ .28 billion	
Health & Human Services ($2.1 billion)		
Mental Health & Public Health (50%)		.4 billion
Human Services		1.2 billion
		Total $2.36 billion
		(45% of $5.3 billion)

INDEX

Made in the USA
Charleston, SC
24 May 2013